ALSO BY MAGGIE & NIGEL PERCY

CARING FOR YOUR ANIMAL COMPANION

THE INTUITIVE, NATURAL WAY TO A HAPPY, HEALTHY PET

MAGGIE PERCY

NIGEL PERCY

For our animal companions,
the finest of friends,
the best of teachers

CONTENTS

PREFACE

- Do you go to the vet for all your pet's health needs, dutifully doing whatever is suggested, even though it seems that you are spending more and more money on your animal's health and seeing less in terms of results?
- Does your animal have stubborn or degenerative disease symptoms that only respond in part to the treatment the vet is offering, and that at a very high price?
- Do you make attempts to train your animal, but find yourself less than thrilled with the results?
- Are there certain patterns of misbehavior that seem so stubborn you can't change them no matter how much effort you put into it?
- Are you beginning to feel frustrated about your animal's behavior, and guilty at how often you lose your temper with your animal companion?
- Does it sometimes feel that although you got a pet because you thought it would lift your spirits and bring joy to your life, that just the opposite is happening?
- Do you avoid talking with your animal and considering its feelings because you have been told that these are silly things to do?

- Do you find yourself wondering whether your animal is angry, upset, guilty or happy, but you aren't sure what to think about animal emotions?
- Do you spend lots of money on attractively packaged foods and treats for your animals that are loaded with preservatives and additives, the way human foods are?
- Does your animal have a weight problem, thin fur, skin allergies or low energy?
- Does your animal seem to be old for his or her age and lacking in vitality?
- Are you dissatisfied with how happy, healthy and well-adjusted your animal is?
- Do you wish you could have a better relationship with your animal friend?

If you have said yes to *ANY* of the above questions, and if you would like to make positive changes in your interactions with your animal companion, there are constructive steps you can take.

- You *CAN* take a more proactive role in the health and training of your animal companion.
- You *CAN* create a good relationship based on communication and understanding.
- You *CAN* help your pet to a happier, healthier life and at the same time have a more rewarding, stress-free relationship.

It's within your power **RIGHT NOW** to do all these things. It doesn't cost a lot of money. It's simple and natural. Just channel the love you have for your animal companion into applying a more balanced, natural approach.

By incorporating an intuitive, natural viewpoint into your relationship with your animal companion, you:

- introduce greater understanding and communication, reducing stress and enhancing enjoyment
- become aware of the invisible influences that affect both you and your pets and take steps to mitigate those that are detrimental to health and well-being
- will make better decisions, which will lead to better results

You've been doing your best all along, but there was a piece missing. This book is intended to lead you step-by-step through the process of adding that missing piece to your current program, thereby improving your results dramatically.

We have spent years not only rescuing and nurturing animals of all kinds in our personal lives; we have spent over ten years working with clients to help them resolve animal problems of all types. In our business Sixth Sense Consulting, we worked with clients all over the world, and it gave us a wealth of experience to draw on.

Maggie has two degrees in Biology that provided excellent background for the scientific aspects of this material, and both of us are certified in a number of energy techniques including Reiki, Spiritual Response Therapy, Spiritual Healing, and Senzar Clearing. We are Master Dowsers who have created a line of courses teaching others how to tap into the power of their Natural Knowing. We are both experts at Emotional Freedom Technique (EFT). In addition, we often use simple solutions involving color, numbers, symbols and crystals to get easy solutions to problems of all kinds.

While we are both lifelong animal enthusiasts, we had problems along the way with our companions. Some of the troubles we have resolved for our personal animal companions are:

- Health issues of all kinds
- Destructive chewing
- Excessive barking
- Inappropriate urination in cats

- Resistance to tacking up in a horse
- Apparent aggression towards children in a dog

For our clients, we have resolved a wide variety of animal issues, often leading to dramatic results. We have retired from individual consultations and are now focusing on teaching others how to do what we do.

The road to success was not straight. It took a lot of effort and commitment. Along the way, new techniques, attitudes and approaches presented themselves and led to solutions. Because of our love of animals and our desire to **ENJOY** them, we studied and persevered.

Sometimes we thought we were beating our heads against the wall, but then eventually we always found a solution. Often it meant studying, reading, learning a new technique or consulting with another professional. But it all added to our knowledge.

We are grateful to the many resources, organizations and helpers who have contributed to our success. Many of them are listed in the Resources section at the end of the book. It is our wish that this book give you a shorter, easier path than we had to happiness with your animal companion.

By enhancing the health and well-being of your animal friend, you may even save money in the long run, but you will certainly help him or her to a longer, more productive and happy life. And isn't that what we all want for our animal companions?

Maggie & Nigel Percy

1

Why Add Intuition?

What's Missing in Your Approach?

INTUITION IS an innate ability we all have, though some have a greater facility using it than others. Our culture denigrates intuition, claiming that science is the only true way to know things about our environment.

Science has contributed tremendously to the progress of our culture, but in doing so it has become something of a religion to most people. Unfortunately, it isn't an infallible source of knowledge and judgment.

Science can only be expected to comment meaningfully on subjects within its area of expertise, but the average person doesn't always realize this limitation. Thus, many intuitive faculties are dismissed as bunk because science can't validate them in the laboratory.

While this book is not meant to attack science or devalue the many contributions of science to our way of life, it will challenge you to think in new ways. It will ask you to use methods that are intuitive, but not scientific, and see what your results are. It will challenge you to rethink your paradigm.

Has your current viewpoint of your relationship with your animal companion brought you great satisfaction, or are you looking for ways to improve that relationship?

If you are open to changing the way you think and do things, this book could well change your relationship with animals for the better. Don't be concerned that you need special talents or abilities to get the most out of this book, or out of your relationship with your animal companion.

We all have the ability to connect with any other living thing. That is the fundamental requirement for establishing a good relationship. This book will provide you with many opportunities to develop and exercise your natural ability to sense your energetic connection with other living things and to become more conscious of the invisible energies in the world around us.

You will have the opportunity to engage your intuitive senses for a more complete interaction with your environment. You can then use that ability to enhance the relationship you have with your dog, cat, horse, rabbit or whatever animal you live or work with.

Invisible Things Affect Your Animal & You

The universe is composed of energy and matter, with energy being the bulk of it. Energy in its many forms is largely undetectable to the five physical senses, except for visible light. X-rays, gamma rays, magnetic and gravity waves exist all around us, and they affect us profoundly, yet we cannot detect them unless we use special scientific instruments.

Most people in our culture believe in these types of invisible energy, but there are many other energies postulated that have not yet been confirmed scientifically, just as X-rays have not always been known. In order to accept that these energies exist, you may have to depart from the strictly scientific viewpoint.

"Energy" as it is used in the non-scientific sense, is something of a vague, over-worked term because it has so many manifestations. Yet it is still useful for describing invisible influences in the physical world.

There are those who believe that all things are connected by energy in some fashion. Quantum physicists and New Age thinkers share that belief. The latter also believe that there are invisible energies in our environment that can affect us for good or bad, just as x-rays can.

DIFFERENT TYPES of Energy

Some energies appear capable of lingering in locations (for example, geographically or in genetic material) for long periods of time, only to become activated by certain conditions, bringing about negative consequences. These energies are not all exactly the same. Each has its unique frequency, manifestation and function.

In addition, many people believe that there are beings that are energetic in form that inhabit this world. Angels, devas and fairies are examples of the names given these "spiritual" beings. Those who believe in angels and nature spirits say that these creatures are an integral part of the natural world, and that if we acknowledge them or ask their help, we can have greater success in our interactions with plant and animal life and with the earth in general.

Other energetic beings are thought to cause havoc with humans. Human discarnates, or ghosts of once-living humans, can linger in the earth plane for long periods of time. Nonhuman entities, of either terrestrial or other origin, are among the spirits that wander the earth causing problems. In 99.9% of the cases, these beings are lost. They do not have an agenda as such. But they are troubled, angry, frustrated, confused and depressed. It is those energies that can contribute to problems with you or your animal friends, as these misplaced beings can attach to physical beings, impacting their emotional and physical health. (Some religions might term this 'possession' or refer to the beings as 'demons', but we find this judgment actually gives the beings power and does not accurately describe them in most cases.)

Everyone is experienced with emotions, and there are many types of emotional energies. Yet science cannot measure love or hate, fear or courage. It can only measure the perceivable effects these emotional energies appear to have on the physical body. Yet we all accept that emotions exist and are powerful energies that can lead to both good and bad actions.

How to Detect Energies?

These diverse "energies" are difficult or impossible to confirm scientifically at this time, but they may be detected using your intuition. Everyone has intuitive senses, but most people have not bothered to use or develop them. Like muscles that have never been used, their intuition is weak and unreliable. But intuition can be strengthened and trained through regular use.

All humans (like all other animals) have an ability to access information intuitively. Using your intuition, you can get answers to questions that you could not answer in any rational way.

Your left brain can only operate rationally, and it does a remarkable job of that. But when you ask it to always provide you with the knowledge you need, it becomes stressed out. Not all answers can be accessed by the rational mind.

Some things can only be known intuitively. Your Inner Voice will speak to you if you listen to it. But you must quiet the left brain in order to hear what your Inner Voice is saying, as long years of disuse have caused it to speak very quietly.

Many people have found the ancient technique of dowsing to be an easy way to access such information intuitively. Dowsing uses your body or other tools to give you answers to your questions.

It is beyond the scope of this book to explore where the answers come from. Though there are many theories, no one can prove exactly where the source of the answers is. While we are not quantum physicists, we feel that since time is a human construct (not real), then all things exist in the 'now'. Therefore all answers exist 'out there'. You just need to access them. And in truth, we believe you go within yourself to get the answers.

In this book we will teach you some simple methods for accessing your intuitive sensing abilities through Dowsing. We will emphasize methods that require no tools. We have spent years strengthening our dowsing abilities, and it has enhanced our relationships with our animal companions in every way possible.

Even though it is not yet widely practiced, Dowsing is a very powerful and effective tool. We believe one reason it is not used a lot is because no one really knows exactly how it works. Strangely, everyone is fine with using cell phones and televisions, even when they have no idea how to construct one. Yet these same people will argue that dowsing can't work, because you can't explain how it does. We're just happy that it works so well!

In spite of the fact that science can't prove dowsing works or explain how it works, the technique dates back probably thousands of years. Dowsing is just one of many intuitive techniques that were considered valid in cultures before the advent of science, which has largely replaced these techniques as a consequence of altering the viewpoint or paradigm of society.

Unfortunately, science is not yet able to do everything dowsing can do. Therefore, to us it makes perfect sense to find a way to use both dowsing **and** science in our relationship with animals.

As you read this material, you will be given the opportunity to experience and experiment with invisible energies of various types. You don't have to be a dowser to do this, nor do you have to have any special talents.

We all have intuitive abilities, as acknowledged by psychologists, but the extent of reliance or belief in them varies from person to person. The next section will examine intuition: what it is, how to measure yours, and how you can use it in your relationships with animals.

How Does Intuition Fit In?

Carl Jung's theory of psychological types states that there are two distinct and very different ways of perceiving. If you use 'sensing', you tend to become aware of things by the use of your five physical senses.

The other process is 'intuition', an indirect perception via the unconscious, which includes ideas or associations added by the unconscious to the perceptions received from outside. (For more details on personality theory, see the Resources section.) While everyone has the capability to perceive in both ways, most people have a natural preference for one method or the other.

People tend to gravitate to jobs and situations that will allow them to use their preferred method of perceiving. This is because to them, their preferred method seems more reliable. By ignoring the less preferred method of perceiving, a person causes it to become weaker through lack of use. This merely reinforces the original belief that it was unreliable.

Intuition is not the favored method of perceiving in our society. 'Women's intuition' and 'hunches' are regarded as unreliable by most people. Even though it is well-documented that the greatest scientific breakthroughs have come through the use of intuition, the scientific establishment and the scientific method emphasize the use of the physical senses over intuitive ones.

· · ·

CAN YOU SEE THINGS DIFFERENTLY?

In this book, you are going to have the chance to exercise your intuition and intuitive senses in general. You will be challenged to sense things in ways other than using your five physical senses. You will be asked to consider that things which are invisible to the eye do indeed exist. You will have the opportunity to get in touch with your feelings and recognize what a powerful force they are for creating your experiences.

This is actually not as alien as it might sound. Remember that everyone has the ability to exercise both a rational *AND* an intuitive viewpoint. Like weak muscles, a poorly used ability may take a bit of practice to build up. But it can be done by anyone.

A TEST: How Intuitive are You?

Next you are going to take a test to see how intuitive you are. If you rate high, then you may find this book fits your attitudes and perspective perfectly. If you score lower, you may find that what is covered in this book challenges you to make big changes in how you think. There is no good or bad score. The overuse of either faculty, sensing or intuitive, can lead to imbalances and negative consequences.

What we are encouraging is a balance between the sensing/rational method, which is emphasized in our culture, and the intuitive way, which is equally valid, but is not highly regarded by our culture.

This test is very simple, but it is important that you take it with the appropriate frame of mind, or your results will be meaningless.

Please select answers that represent your own personal preference. Do NOT select answers that you feel are right based on anything external to you, such as what you do to succeed at work, what is expected of you from friends and family, or what society thinks you should value.

These external values are often different from personal preferences, and you will not get an accurate score if you select answers based on what you think you SHOULD like or prefer, or what you HAVE to do to survive in society.

For more information on personality testing, see the Books on Personality Theory section for titles and links.

Answer 'yes' or 'no' to the following questions :

1. Do you prefer getting an idea of the 'big picture' rather than having to get bogged down in tiny details? (For example, do you tend to skip reading instructions unless you absolutely have to?)

2. Do you frequently skip logical steps in the thinking process, arriving at conclusions with the help of insight and hunches? (If so, you probably find it tedious to listen to what seem like obvious step-by-step presentations, because you usually see what is being aimed at in advance.)

3. Do you tend to view relationships optimistically, seeing what is possible rather than what is really there now?

4. When at work, do you like to learn new skills and new ways of doing things, rather than always using the 'tried and true' methods that have sufficed in the past?

5. Do the words/phrases 'sixth sense, theoretical, future possibilities' and 'insights' attract you more than the words/phrases 'facts, practical, what is real' and 'the five senses'?

6. Do you enjoy reading for pleasure and working with computers?

7. When traveling in a new place, do you tend to get general impressions about your surroundings, rather than noting details? Do you tend to give directions that relate to landmarks, partly because you find yourself bemused about compass directions when in a strange place (e.g., 'travel 6 blocks north' seems absurd to you)?

8. Do you feel that whatever is, can be better or different, and thus you find yourself focusing on possibilities for improving things?

9. Do you sometimes or often make decisions based purely on a gut feeling, and later find out you were right?

SCORING the Test

Each 'yes' answer represents a choice for the use of intuition over the five senses. The higher your score, the greater your preference for the intuitive senses.

This does not mean you exercise your intuition to an extreme, but that it is your preference. You may behave differently in your relationships or at work than is your preference, but this test is meant to demonstrate your natural inclinations, which may also be reflected in your perceived abilities and experiences with respect to intuition.

Indeed, if you have very many or very few 'yes' answers, it would be wise of you to beware of exercising your preference too much, whichever that is. We all have both intuitive and physical sensing capabilities, and it is best to combine the two types of methods of interacting with the environment, rather than relying on one alone.

In this book, you will be asked to exercise your intuition, which we believe will aid you in developing a better relationship with your animal companions. In our culture, intuition has been devalued to the point that many people don't trust their gut feelings. We believe that if you have a viewpoint that incorporates intuition, you will have a more balanced and successful relationship with animals.

2

Choosing A Pet

Avoid the Big Mistake: Choose Your Friend Wisely

MANY PEOPLE GIVE little time and thought to this part of the process of forming a relationship with an animal. You can greatly increase your chances of a happy relationship with your pet if you devote some care to your choice of animal companion.

Animals can live from 2 to over 30 years, depending on species. Each species has its own particular needs in terms of diet, exercise, grooming, training and other care. Some animals are highly expensive to own, while others are not.

Animals have lifestyles and personalities that need to be a good match with their caretaker, or trouble ensues. In a multiple-pet household, it is important to consider how the different animals will get along when you intend to add a new member. It is also important to consider the other human members of your family when choosing a pet. Safety and compatibility are two important factors.

How often have you or an acquaintance failed to consider these or other important facts about pet ownership, only to experience disaster or disappointment as a result?

There are many factors to consider when you are choosing an animal friend. This section will not only cover as many of these as possible, it will encourage you to incorporate both intuitive and rational methods to prepare for and make your choice of animal companion.

Tests

Before you decide what pet you want to get, you need to ask yourself some questions about factors that may affect your choice of animal. The first questionnaire deals with the rational side of pet choice, and the second, with the intuitive aspects. Both self-tests may be found in the Appendices.

RATIONAL CHOICE

The following questions are designed to make you think about your choice of an animal companion in a logical, reasonable way. It is critical that you answer these questions honestly for best results.

Comments after each question are to help you see why these subjects are important to your relationship with your pet.

1. *Do you spend a lot of time outdoors participating in activities that are very physical?* If you enjoy outdoor activities, you may prefer an animal that can join you in your interests. A horse or dog would possibly be a good choice.

2. *Are you more of an indoors person, who likes to read and watch TV in your spare time?* Anything from a fish, turtle or bird to a cat or possibly a dog might serve your needs.

3. *Are you living in rented space where you have to be extra cautious about damage?* Animals that live in cages, like birds, guinea pigs, rabbits, hamsters, fish and reptiles may be best for you.

4. *Do you live in a high density location, like a city apartment complex, or a rural setting with a great deal of open space?* Animals like dogs, horses and even cats need a fair amount of exercise to be healthy. Consider how much you can provide where you live.

5. *Is your living space very casually appointed, with secondhand furniture, or do you have fine antiques and valuable artifacts?* Puppies, kittens, dogs and cats can be terribly destructive. If that will bother you, then perhaps a bird, fish, reptile or other caged animal will be a safe bet for you.

6. *Do you spend a lot of time at home during the day? During the evening? On weekends?* The more time you spend, the better. Any type of animal needs your attention. If you aren't home much, then you probably shouldn't have an animal dependent on you, unless it is something very simple like fish or reptiles.

7. *Do you live with other people? If so, what sex and ages are they?* Small children are not always compatible with dogs and cats. Small dogs are not necessarily safer for children than large ones. In fact, in my experience, the opposite is often true. Much supervision and training (of animals *and* children) is required when small children live with animals. Don't get a pet if you can't commit to that.

8. *Does everyone you live with like animals? Are there any allergies to animals, fear of animals, or other reasons that would make a pet an issue?* You must consider everyone in your living space when you are getting a pet. Check phobias and allergies as well as personal preferences before acquiring your companion animal. If you have a long-standing animal relationship that is in conflict with a current boy or girlfriend, then maybe you need to reconsider the relationship (with the boyfriend/girlfriend).

9. *Will this animal be the only pet you have, or do you have others? If others, what type are they? How do they like other animals of this type? How can you be sure?* Consider the feelings of your other animal companions before you get a new friend. Older dogs and cats often feel put upon when a new kitten or puppy comes along. Sometimes, however, it gives them a new lease on life. It is wise to consult the pet directly for their preference. If you can't ask them yourself, hire an animal communicator to ask them.

10. *Is your weather sunny, warm and dry, or cold and wet? Is it extreme in any way?* If your animal has to live outdoors (this is not desirable for many) or spend a lot of time outdoors with you, then you need to make sure it is suited to your climate. A Newfoundland is not bred for desert weather, nor is a greyhound likely to enjoy Alaskan winters. Find out about the climate that best suits the breed of animal you are considering. Most likely, this will be the climate they originally were bred to live and work in.

11. *What do you like about the idea of having a pet? Have you lived with this type of animal before (the one you are considering getting)? Does this type of animal lend itself to your dream?* Examine your reasons for getting a pet. Make sure they are grounded in reality and that you are compatible with this type of animal.

12. *How much time do you have each day to devote to training, grooming, feeding, exercising and playing with your animal friend? Do you have time to take it for health care when needed?* Don't get a long-haired cat or dog if you don't want to brush it. Don't get a shedding dog if hair all over the place bothers you. Dogs and cats and horses require training. Don't get one if you don't have the time, interest and money to do so.

13. *Do you like doing things for an animal like brushing, nail trimming, tooth brushing, bathing, hair trimming, etc?* Even if you have the time and money to groom and train your pet, is it something you really want to do? If not, reconsider your choice.

14. *Have you done any research on the health requirements, training needs and behavior of this type of animal? If so, how much?* Educate yourself about the species of animal you are thinking of purchasing. You might be amazed at the amount of care most animals need. It isn't enough to just feed and walk a dog. Animals require dental care, grooming, training, exercise and love. Horses in particular are very labor-intensive to maintain properly.

15. *Are you a laid-back type of person or a perfectionist? How easily irritated are you by messes, noise, frustration and accidents that involve damage to things you value?* If you are a highly irritable person, then a dog or cat probably isn't for you. They will try your patience too much. Get some help with your challenges before acquiring an animal that might aggravate you.

16. *Are you demonstrative and affectionate or more reserved? Are you embarrassed to talk out loud to your animal friend, even in private?* The more intelligent an animal, the more important it is for you to talk with it and express yourself in some fashion. More reserved people might prefer animals that don't demand interaction as much as dogs and cats do.

17. *Do you feel like animals have emotions somewhat like humans? Do you empathize with them easily? Are you a nurturing person?* You may be an excellent person to help foster homeless animals or raise orphaned ones. Animals that seek interaction may be better suited to you than independent ones.

18. *What are your finances like? Do you have more than enough money to provide good quality food, training, grooming, health care and boarding when required?* If you're not sure, then you aren't ready to take on the responsibility of a dependent animal. It always costs more than you think to take on a dependent if you intend to do things right. Make sure you can commit to doing what an animal needs to have a healthy lifestyle. If money is tight, you can still own a small animal and enjoy the benefits of pet ownership, but you may want to avoid dogs, cats and horses, which are higher maintenance animals.

19. *Are you prepared for a long-term commitment to this animal? Do you know the average life span? Can you see yourself with this animal for that long?* DON'T get an animal thinking you can always give her away or sell her if you change your mind. Do your best to commit to caring for an animal for life, but be aware that things sometimes happen that change your abilities to do so. Don't put a burden on yourself, but don't be thoughtless, either. Going from home to home or owner to owner is very taxing and stressful on an animal. Plan on keeping your animal for her entire life if possible. Don't treat her like a piece of furniture.

20. *Are you easily provoked to physical violence when angry?* If so, it would be best **NOT** to acquire an animal companion. Instead, seek counseling to learn to express your anger in other ways before bringing an animal into your life.

21. *Are you under a lot of stress in your life at the current time?* If so, it is **NOT** advisable to get a pet at this time. There are many ways to work on stress management that can reduce your stress levels, but getting a pet is not one of them if your stress level is high. There is too great a risk that your animal will either contribute to the stress you feel by her demands on your time and money, or that you will use your animal as an outlet for stress-related emotions that are not healthy for the animal. Furthermore, animals always reflect our current conditions, and a stressed-out pet can be destructive or ill.

INTUITIVE CHOOSING

You will be asked to think about some subjects that relate to your choice of animal friend from an intuitive view point. This will not be as linear and straightforward as the previous exercise, because it is intuitive.

As with the other evaluation, there are no right or wrong answers. These questions are merely to motivate you to think intuitively about the decision you are getting ready to make.

1. *How do you relate to animals?*

Have they always been a part of your life, so that you feel incomplete without one by your side? Some people are animal people. Still others go beyond that, and are cat persons, or horse persons, based on their favorite species. Think about how you feel about animals. Have you always felt that way? Are they important to you, or can you live happily without them? Does your desire to have a pet stem from a driving **NEED** or simply a wish to have a companion? Your actual answer is not as important as your motivation for it. Think carefully about how you feel about animals. Don't get a pet just because you always have had one, or because you are desperately lonely. Make sure you actively want to have an animal in your life. Pets are not child or significant other-substitutes. They are animal friends.

2. *Why are you choosing this particular type of animal?*

Have you always wanted a black horse or a yellow dog? Is it because your friend has a great animal that you like, and you want to have a similar relationship? Are you being forced to adopt an animal by your children or spouse, but you don't really want one? Is a relative or friend trying to convince you to take on their animal, because they no longer need, want or can care for it? 'Why' is an important question. Sometimes it is hard to be honest. Listen to your heart. What does it tell you about getting an animal companion?

3. *Examine your feelings about this decision.*

Are you getting a pet out of guilt, obligation, pressure or envy? Don't do it. Do you feel calm about doing this? Excited? Afraid? Examine all your feelings about this choice. You will probably have many. A feeling solely of excitement may mean you are doing this for the emotional high it gives you. Make sure you feel grounded, calm and peaceful about the decision as well. Examine any feelings of fear, and make sure they aren't a signal from your intuition that this is the wrong time, place or choice for you. A tight, churning feeling in your gut usually means you shouldn't do it.

4. *Are you rushing to make this purchase?*

If so, you may be subconsciously trying to override your intuitive feelings that this is not a good choice. Slow down, take your time. Listen to your heart and pay attention to the signs your body gives you about what you are considering.

5. *Have you always wanted this particular type of animal in your life, or is it a sudden new interest?*

Be careful either way. Get in touch with your feelings about this decision. Are you trying to make a childhood dream come true? Why? Don't get a pony just because you are mad your parents never got you one. Maybe they were right. Even if they weren't, they were doing the best they could at the time. If your interest is recent, are you sure it isn't some fad you are jumping on the bandwagon to join?

6. *Do you resonate with this particular type of animal?*

Does everything about it 'ring true' to you? Can you easily see yourself living with this animal as a companion for many years? Do you have a strong desire to interact with this animal: ride your horse, play with a dog, stroke a cat? Good. You are on the right track.

TYPES OF PETS

If you make a purely rational choice of pet, you may find yourself lacking the enthusiasm to take care of him or her, because your 'heart' wasn't in the decision, and that is needed so you can bond with your friend. However, if you make a purely emotional decision, you may end up with an animal that doesn't fit you at all, leading to sadness and eventually to getting rid of him.

Combine both your head and your heart in equal measures to get the right animal for you.

What are some of the types of animals you might consider as your new friend? Let's start with small, simple animals and work our way up.

. . .

FISH

Fish can be very interesting animals to live with. They live in their own habitat and don't eat your furniture or mess on the carpet. You don't have to train them if you don't have time, and they won't make you feel guilty if you don't play with them every day. You can invest as little or as much in this type of animal as you wish.

Fish have the distinction of being excellent feng shui, drawing in wealth and prosperity if placed appropriately in your living space and cared for excellently.

BIRDS

Birds add the element of sound to your environment. Many species are actually quite intelligent, like some parrots, and live a long time. They can be trained to do many things, and if treated like the intelligent beings they are, they can bond closely with their humans. They are also beautiful animals.

As with reptiles, you may choose to let them have some freedom from their cage under supervision, with terrific results. We had two chickens for pets, and one in particular was delightful and affectionate.

REPTILES AND AMPHIBIANS

Reptiles and amphibians are interesting pets. Reptiles can be reminiscent of little dinosaurs, thus tickling the fancy of children who like these ancient animals. Although fairly easy to keep and care for, it is important to understand the requirements of these animals, which are 'cold-blooded' like fish.

. . .

SMALL MAMMALS

Small mammals like mice, hamsters, guinea pigs and gerbils can be excellent friends for people who for one reason or other can't have larger pets, but want an animal they can pet and talk to and play with.

These animals can become as friendly as you want them to be, depending on the time you take to tame them. They stay safely in their cage until you want to remove them at playtime. Older adults and responsible children can enjoy these exceptional pets.

Rabbits

Rabbits are in a class of their own. They are too big to be small mammals, but too small to be big ones. The cages most rabbits live in amount to jail cells that are stressful and harmful to their health. These animals need lots of space, and can be very loving if cared for and handled properly.

Although their propensity to chew usually means they need to be restricted/supervised closely, they love supervised play sessions running around the house stretching their legs, jumping up and down on beds. These can be great pets for people who can't have dogs or cats in their living space for whatever reason. They can be litter trained rather easily in most cases. They are also capable of being very affectionate.

CATS

Cats are now the most popular pet in the U.S. They require less attention than dogs, which makes them a favorite of apartment dwellers. However, they can be just as loving as dogs if they are given the same type of attention. The fact that they can be litter trained makes them lower maintenance than dogs.

• • •

Dogs

Nothing is quite like a dog for companionship. They love you no matter what you do or say. They are the most loyal creatures you can imagine. Their wonderful qualities demand reciprocation.

Dogs are not for those who are never home, who tie them outside all the time, or who can't be bothered to interact with them on a regular basis. Having a dog is a lot like having a child. They are a lot of work, but they can return your investment many times over.

If you are thinking of having a dog as a pet, plan on taking time to train it properly. Dogs do not automatically know how to behave in human company or homes. You will enjoy your dog more if you train it.

Horses

Horse ownership is not for the faint of heart. Most people have to board their horse away from home. The bills for health care, feeding, boarding, shoeing, training and tack can pile up fast, so finances are a big factor in horse ownership. If you are financially comfortable and you enjoy having an animal to nurture, then a horse may be right for you.

You must be aware of the horse's prey animal mentality and understand it will exhibit greater timidity as a rule than predatory animals such as dogs and cats. Green riders should never buy green horses, as that can be a safety issue. With proper experience, patience, nutrition and training, a horse can become a tremendous companion for traveling outdoors.

As with all animals, we recommend that you do not get a horse unless you have the time to train it, ride it and care for it. They are not just big yard ornaments. Too many people treat horses like pieces of furniture, adding to their emotional baggage. And added emotional baggage leads to health and behavior issues.

. . .

OTHERS

Obviously, there are many types of animals not covered here. Some people have livestock as pets with very good results.

Exotics frequently do *NOT* make satisfactory pets. The best place for wild animals is the wild. However, sometimes things happen and wild animals require rehabilitation. Under certain circumstances, they may not be able to return to the wild.

Only people who have the proper abilities should attempt to care for and keep wild animals. It is always wise to consult local laws in this regard. There are usually organizations or individuals who help rehabilitate wild animals, especially birds and mammals. There is more on The Rescue Animal in a later section.

Where to Find Your Animal Companion

Depending on where you live, there may be a variety of sources for the animal you intend to acquire. This section will address some of the typical sources, although not all apply to every type of animal.

Breeders

There are professional breeders and amateur breeders. A professional breeder is perhaps a better bet as a source for a pet than an amateur breeder, simply because professionals have a reputation to uphold.

Unfortunately, because money is a factor in any breeding program, you will have to research carefully and use your intuition to select a good source.

Most breeding standards and practices leave much to be desired, as they are geared towards breeding for looks or a few particular traits, and money is almost always a factor, so some breeders give the least health care and the cheapest nutrition they can to increase their profit margin. In some cases these decisions are made out of ignorance rather than greed, but the results are just as bad.

Use your head and research breeders. Follow your instinct when you visit a breeder. Get a feel for them and their operation, values and ethics.

Many who consider themselves professional breeders because they sell animals they have bred are in reality amateurs who don't know much about the breed, health care, nutrition or training.

Others are caring and experienced people who share their knowledge generously with those who purchase animals from them.

If the breeder has a contract, especially one that has a contingency for taking the animal back if you can't keep it or decide you don't like it, this is a sign that they care about the welfare of the animal.

Pet Stores

The local pet store is a convenient place to get a pet, and for some people, it may be the only place. Just bear in mind that you are probably not getting the most well-bred animal if you buy there, especially a kitten or puppy.

Professional breeders don't usually provide animals for pet stores. They often have contracts with prospective 'parents' and have a policy of return that is rather flexible.

Pet stores don't usually check out prospective buyers, except to see if they have enough money to pay for the animal. They have a different agenda, and their stock will reflect that. However, there are many nice, well-kept pet stores owned by ethical people.

Once again, you have to use your head and research and ask questions, and then follow your heart and your gut instinct. Many chain pet stores now only offer small animals for sale.

. . .

RESCUE ORGANIZATIONS

If you get an animal here, it will cost you less up front than if you buy from a breeder or pet store. However, be aware that you will need to spend more time and money on animals obtained here than those who have had a good start in life. (Although in some cases, other sources can be lumped into this category as well.)

Animals that have been rejected, abused or malnourished have special needs due to the poor state of their health and immune system. Furthermore, they have emotional challenges due to the unhappy events of their early lives.

While it is admirable to 'save' an animal by adopting from a shelter, it is wise to educate yourself as to how best to rehabilitate such an animal, and once again, follow your intuition concerning your choice.

An advantage of getting a hybrid animal is that often their inherent health is quite good due to their mixed breeding, so once you get them healthy they may stay that way more easily. Our experience has been that rescued animals take at least a year of extra care to become fully healthy, more often two years, depending on circumstances.

There are many breed-specific rescue organizations, so if you want a purebred dog or cat, check them out.

Individuals

Sometimes a friend or relative has an animal they need to get rid of. Or maybe you have seen an ad in the paper from a person who is moving and has to give away their cat.

Ask a lot of questions here as elsewhere, and visit the person in their home. See the environment they provide for their animal, and how they interact. Listen to your heart when they give you their reasons for selling their pet. If things don't look or feel right, move on.

Finding an Animal

"He followed me home. Can I keep him?" This is covered in more detail in the next section. Sometimes animals find us or choose us. If this happens to you, you will have to decide what you have been chosen for. Are you meant to adopt this animal or do you know just the right person for him?

Being Given an Animal as a Gift

This is perhaps the 'worst' way to acquire an animal companion, although in a later section we will talk about believing that all things happen for a purpose. However, being given a pet does not allow you to exercise either your brain or your heart. Someone else chooses for you. It is unlikely anyone can know you that well.

Don't give someone an animal as a gift unless they have told you exactly which one they want and where to get it from. Don't feel you have to keep an animal that someone gives you as a gift unless you really want it.

Dumping Animals

Shortly after Easter one year we found two tiny ducklings in the creek below our house. We brought them in and tried to help them (my best friend was a veterinarian, and she happened to be visiting, so she helped as well), but they died from exposure. No doubt someone got them for Easter and didn't want to keep them. They rationalized that ducks live in the wild. Perhaps they were too ignorant to know that ducklings in the wild live with their parents.

My rabbit Moki came to me in the same way. The week after Easter one year, I found her loose in our neighborhood. None of the neighbors nearby would admit that she was theirs, so I kept her for the next nine years. Domestic rabbits don't stand much of a chance outdoors on their own, as they are not bred for living outside and foraging for their own food and shelter. They probably can't get enough of the right kind of food in the wild to maintain health.

People can be pretty cruel to animals through this type of ignorance. Educate yourself. Ask for help. DON'T DUMP AN UNWANTED ANIMAL.

Nigel and I had been living in our home in Cottonwood, AZ for about a year. He loved cats even more than I do, and we had decided that our dog India needed some companionship, as our other dog Roger wasn't too sociable with other animals. So we planned to get a cat as a friend for her. We decided it made more sense to wait until summer, as we had a week-long trip to California planned for early July, and figured the fewer animals we left behind, the better.

Fate has a way of making things happen differently than you plan. We got a call in April from a friend who said the local shelter needed foster parents for kittens and their moms. We went and got a mother and her six kittens, and voila!, we ended up keeping the mother and one kitten. That was one more cat than we planned on, and not at the time we had selected.

However, everything turned out so well that we are thrilled we did. The cats loved the dogs, and India was a happy girl with her 'herd' of cats. Put your intention out there, and then be guided by what the Universe offers you in return. It is often better than what you planned on. However, if you don't keep it, make sure you find a safe person or organization to care for it.

Now that you have spent a lot of time reading about how to make a good choice of animal companion, go to the next chapter where we will discuss whether you are really making a choice at all.

Is Choice Illusion or Reality?

Thinking Rationally

Now that you have been given lots of things to think about concerning your choice of animal friend, it is time to look at the possibility that choice is merely an illusion.

"Wait a minute!" you say. "How can that be?" Or maybe you are thinking, "Why did you go to such trouble telling me how to choose if the choice isn't really mine?"

The traditional way of thinking goes that you can do your research on the animal you want, check out sources, go look at animals, then make a choice. You have therefore controlled every step of the process, and you will get the animal of your dreams.

But it doesn't work like that, does it? Even if you follow all the suggestions of the previous sections, you may still end up with something other than what you envisioned.

Normally, if things don't turn out as you plan, you may think you made a mistake, or that someone lied to you. Or perhaps you just chalk it up to bad luck. Whatever excuse you give, it all amounts to the belief that 'if only' you or someone had done something differently, all would be well, and you would have your dream.

Unhappiness and stress result when we are convinced that through rational thought we should be able to control the outcome of any situation, because it just isn't possible.

THINKING INTUITIVELY

Try looking at things in a more natural, intuitive fashion. Life is complex, and you can't control everything in it. It isn't linear. You don't follow steps 1 through 9 and end up at 10. It's more like a network of connecting lines that form a web. Frequently you get sidetracked and end up at -5, or even 20. Sometimes you end up at 10, but mostly, you don't.

This doesn't mean you should discard the work you did in the earlier sections. You just have to know what you want, do your research and give careful consideration to what your instincts tell you.

In other words, be open to the possibility that something better may come to you than what you planned. That is the beauty of trusting your intuition.

Let Go of Control

You decide that you want a particular type of animal for your companion, and you do the best you can to follow your heart and mind. Be open to what is best for you. What you thought would make you happy may not be the best choice. Don't wear blinders. Check out the unexpected leads or suggestions made by friends and strangers. Notice the interesting article in the paper or magazine that relates to your search. Maybe it has a place or person you need to check out.

Be aware if you seem blocked every step of the way. That may be a message from your intuition saying, "Don't do it". Don't try to control every step of this process. Ask for guidance, and you will receive it. By adding intuition to the process, you will find the results give you greater happiness and satisfaction.

Summary

In summary, here are some important things to do before you go out and purchase an animal companion. For best and happiest results, use both your rational and intuitive faculties for gathering information about which is the best animal for you to have.

1. Quiz yourself on factors that will affect your compatibility

with the animal type you wish to have. Select an animal that fits into your lifestyle and complements your personality.

2. Check out other important factors such as how other humans and animals in your family may be affected by a new addition. Don't assume you can 'fix' things later.

3. Educate yourself on the maintenance and training requirements of your prospective pet, and read about the normal personality traits of the breed. You don't want surprises.

4. Don't adopt a new animal friend if you are under terrible stress at this time, or if you have challenges controlling your temper. It will only make things worse.

5. Give very careful and serious consideration to your feelings about animals, this type in particular, and why you want to acquire one.

6. Visualize your image of how you and your new friend will relate. Compare that with your known habits and values. Does it feel 'doable'? If so, that's great.

7. Do you have a really good but solidly grounded feeling about this decision? Terrific. Or do you have knots in your stomach, trepidation or a sense of being rushed to get this done and over with? Is everything going wrong in your plan? Your intuition may be telling you to back up, back off or postpone your decision. Follow it.

3

Animal Communication

You are an Animal Communicator!

JUST BECAUSE OTHER people have obvious psychic gifts and can talk fluently with animals over long distances is no reason for you to say you can't communicate with animals. While there are specialists who do this for a living, you already are a bona fide animal communicator.

In this section you will see how you communicate with your animal companions every day in ways you may not even have thought of. In the next section, you will learn ways to make that communication conscious, and thus, more effective.

The word "communicate" means to make known; to have an interchange, as of thoughts or ideas; to be connected. Communication takes many forms: verbal, written, symbolic and body language are a few.

Your animal can't read and write, but you communicate a lot to her through symbolic and verbal communication and body language.

Some people even believe there is a telepathic link between humans and their animals.

Let's examine the ways in which you are already communicating with your pet.

Verbal Communication

Everyone is aware that they can communicate with their animal through words. Depending on the species of animal you have, you may not believe your animal understands much of what you say to it. This is partly because our scientifically-oriented culture tends to disbelieve things that haven't been proven scientifically, that is, through the physical senses.

However, you are aware that your animal responds to what you say. Words are the most obvious way of communicating with your animal companion. The more you talk to your animal, the bigger her passive vocabulary gets. It doesn't matter what kind of animal you have, you will benefit from talking to her as much as possible. This is especially true of when you leave her to go somewhere, or when something is happening that she may not like or understand, like at the vet's.

Don't be afraid that someone will make fun of you. Doing this will help you bond better with your pet and enhance understanding. The same is true of young children, so this isn't such a strange suggestion.

As you talk to your animal, imagine what she is getting out of your speech. Try to send her pictures of what you are talking about. Animals can be telepathic, and this can aid them in learning language.

Tone of Voice & Body Language

The tone of your voice and your body language give valuable cues to the animals in your life. Dogs will often look guilty even when they haven't done anything, just because the owner has a certain tone of voice and aggressive, angry behavior. If you don't believe it, try it on your dog. But then be sure to apologize to her.

Touch

Touch can be either positive or negative, depending on the intentions and emotions behind it.

As mentioned earlier, stroking, grooming or touching your animal in positive, healing ways communicates your love as well as enhancing health. Most animals require regular brushing or combing. If you take time to make grooming a time of bonding rather than a chore, you will strengthen your relationship.

Some animals don't like grooming. For them, other forms of touch therapy may be used. Massage is becoming very popular with animal owners. It is an excellent way of relaxing the animal and aiding circulation, among other things. You don't have to be a professional to give your animal a massage.

Or perhaps you are interested in learning TTouch, Reiki or Bowen techniques. There are many healing therapies that involve touch, and they are highly beneficial to animals and communicate your love for them.

Play

Taking the time to play with your animal regularly communicates your love to him. Whether you have a dog, cat, rabbit, horse or turtle, take time out every day if possible to play with your animal in some fashion.

For simpler animals, a supervised run around the house might be considered entertaining and exciting. For others, more complex forms of play may be used. Riding your horse regularly is one of the best gifts you can give him and about the best way to communicate to him that you care. Don't be too busy to play with your friend. It is good for you, too!

COMMUNICATION THROUGH OBJECTS

Objects can take on meanings for animals, and those meanings can be either positive or negative. A favorite toy will bring out playful behavior in your cat, but a rolled up newspaper may make your dog slink out of the room guiltily.

How your animal reacts to those objects may depend on what association he makes with them. If your horse's saddle doesn't fit, he may behave negatively when you bring it out. So the object may evoke feelings about pain or a health issue.

Remember to look at things through your animal's eyes and imagine what they are trying to say to you. An animal can't tell you in words that it hurts, so he tells you in actions.

Always assume an animal's actions are appropriate given the situation. It is up to you to find out what the animal is trying to tell you. After all, you are supposed to be the smarter of the two!

BEHAVIOR

Just as animals use behavior to communicate with us and each other, they learn from us through our behavior. Animals are excellent at detecting patterns, and you may wonder how they can tell time so precisely. It is pretty amazing how they know within minutes when dinner time is or when you have to get up in the morning.

When I was in college, I rescued a kitten. Each semester, she learned my class schedule. She would only wake me up early on days I had an 8 a.m. class. She learned this by observing when I encouraged her waking me up early and when I didn't. She quickly adapted each semester to the new schedule.

If you pay attention to your behavior, you may be able to see what and how it is communicating with your animal. Most animals are sensitive to negativity, even if it isn't directed at them. Negativity will raise the stress level of your animal, leading to health and behavior issues.

Do what you can to create a harmonious environment for your animal friend. It will enhance your health and well-being also.

You also "tell" your animal things through your behavior. Animals assess patterns rather well, and learn to anticipate your next move based on past experience. This is why your dog expects you to walk him after you eat breakfast, because that is your habit.

TELEPATHY

You may not believe in telepathy as such, but many people have stories of how psychic their pets appear to be. Their ability to know what is going on often surpasses their passive vocabulary or ability to read behavior.

Although it hasn't been demonstrated scientifically, there are many anecdotes about animal telepathy. It makes sense to imagine that since they lack a complex verbal ability, many species could communicate subtly using thought energy.

We are all aware of the amazing feats that animals perform using the physical senses. Their hearing and smell are incredible. Why couldn't they have other senses that are equally amazing and surpass what we have, such as the ability to communicate telepathically? Anyone who puts out wild bird seed can tell you that birds seem to find out unusually fast about the new food source, as if they had some kind of mental link.

From my own experience, I have found that among our cats, some are more tuned in to me than others. Jack in particular seems to know what I am thinking. On the rare occasion I decide to put out catnip, he comes running from wherever he is, usually before I even get the jar out of the cupboard. If I decide to groom the cats who want it, he rockets through the pet door before I even get settled with the cat brush. And when I wonder where he is, he often shows up as if I had called him. I have also found that when one of our dogs is barking outside at night, I am sometimes able to 'call' him or her into the house telepathically.

COMMUNICATING CONSCIOUSLY

Now that you realize how many ways there are to communicate and connect with your animal companion, let's look at ways to improve how you do that. The goal of this section is to convince you to communicate with your pet consciously.

You already communicate in the ways mentioned in the previous section, but you probably aren't using them in a conscious fashion. Furthermore, you probably aren't considering things from your animal's point of view, and thus, you aren't communicating as effectively as you could.

The messages you give looking at things from another's point of view is the natural, intuitive way. This does not necessarily mean empathy. Being aware of her viewpoint is not the same thing as feeling the same as your pet does.

When it comes to communicating, we want to suggest you try to imagine how your animal regards and understands what you are saying or doing. What exactly do your words and deeds tell your animal companion?

Animals and children do not think like adult humans, and if you want to avoid misunderstanding, you need to be aware of their viewpoint. For example, if your dog runs out into the road instead of coming when you call it, you might be so upset and afraid for its health that when you finally run the little critter down or he finally comes back, you either yell at him or smack him to release your negative energies.

The same thing often happens with small children. As you are yelling, you communicate great negativity and displeasure. However, what are you displeased about? Aren't you really upset because you were afraid your animal would be hurt? Isn't that why you really wanted to spank him?

Even if this is not the case, does the animal understand that you are punishing him for his earlier transgression, or does he feel you are punishing him because he finally returned or allowed you to catch him?

Punishment has to follow the wrongful behavior immediately to be effective. In this example, since it didn't, you will train your dog **NOT** to come, because the last thing he did before the punishment was to return to you or allow you to catch him. This is contrary to your goals, and will also damage the trust your animal has in you, as well as confuse the heck out of him.

THINKING DIFFERENTLY

It takes effort to think like an animal, but if you remember that they are not as verbal as humans, and that they are reading your mood and actions and correlating them with what they just did, you will have better results in communicating your desires to your animal successfully.

Animals are also quite literal. Many people get annoyed when their dog won't stay when they say `sit'. However, unless you have trained the dog to `stay' whenever you say `sit', your dog is right and you are wrong. `Sit' only means sit for a second, while `stay' means stay put for a while or until released. Animals will challenge you to listen to what you say and see what is sloppy or misleading about it, if you look at things through their eyes. They are also like children in being able to take advantage of weakness or inconsistency in behavior.

Assume your animal has always responded correctly to you. Look at your own words, behavior or training methods for possible causes of the perceived misbehavior.

Let's look at the different methods of communicating we discussed in the last section and see how they can be used to best advantage in your relationship with animals.

STAY Positive

When talking to your animal, make sure you aren't negative in any way. Don't call your animal names or threaten her. Praise her and compliment her as much as possible. Like a small child, animals can have self-esteem issues and can absorb negative feelings, thus becoming the very thing you don't want them to be.

Don't tell your animal what you **DON'T** want her to do. Tell her, show her and visualize for her what you **DO** want her to do. The word 'not' is lost in the command, "Don't eat the couch while I'm gone." In telling your animal this, you make her focus on what you don't want her to do, which is counterproductive.

Your anxieties and fears and your imaginings about the torn up couch can be communicated to your animal in a way that becomes a self-fulfilling prophecy. There will be more on this in a later section.

TOUGH LOVE

Our cat Cleo raised six kittens when she was barely five pounds in weight herself, having been caught in the wild while pregnant and feral. In spite of poor nutrition and the trauma of being captured and caged, Cleo was a perfect mother.

We adopted her and her kitten Tuffy. She always reprimanded Tuffy by licking her very strongly. It was a comical sight, as it stopped the kitten from doing the unwanted behavior, but did it in a loving fashion. Perhaps that is where the expression "get a lickin" comes from!

PUNISHMENT

It should go without saying that touch can be negative if you strike your animal in anger. Animals understand aggression, and in most cases, it will damage your relationship. Rarely is it appropriate to hit an animal, and then, never in anger.

It takes great talent to learn how to administer physical punishment, for example, the way a mother dog does. It requires timing, good sense and a very stable personality, and it must be delivered quickly, with love, and with just the right degree of force to communicate without harming. Most people aren't capable of doing this without a lot of training.

TRUST Yourself

Learning to communicate this way or in other advanced ways challenges you to engage your intuitive senses rather than the physical, and just *KNOW* what the animal is telling you.

Practice being open to what your animal is saying. Don't analyze her behavior or think about what she is doing. Just relax and when she looks at you, be open to knowing what she wants to say to you. You may be amazed to discover that you know whether she is concerned about going outside, having a meal or just wants a cuddle.

Too often, we ignore the subtle cues our animals send us that communicate so much. Take the time to look at and listen to what your animal is saying. You will be surprised to find you don't have to wait until she starts barking to get the message.

• • •

ADVANCED ANIMAL COMMUNICATION

In the Appendix, you will find a method for advanced animal communication that you might enjoy practicing. It is the first method Maggie learned, from a good friend who mentored her in horse nutrition, training and care. It's a method anyone can learn to do. How long it takes you to become proficient depends on native talent and practice. We highly recommend you learn it.

SUMMARY

1. Look at things from your animal's viewpoint whenever possible.

Your current way of communicating may be failing to express your actual thoughts and feelings to your animal friend, because he or she doesn't understand your viewpoint.

2. Talk to your animal.

Let him or her know what you are doing and why.

3. Play with your animal friend.

Play is a good way to connect.

4. Use touch to enhance your relationship.

Simple massage, grooming and gentle stroking are excellent. Even better, learn a touch therapy like TTouch or Reiki.

5. Send your animal pictures of what you want him or her to do, not what you DON'T want.

Regularly use thoughts to communicate with your animal. Ask for confirmation that what you say is understood.

6. Practice a more challenging intuitive method of communicating with your animal companion.

The more you practice, the better you will get.

7. Be patient.

Evaluate your progress over the long term rather than on a daily basis.

8. Ask for help from the angels and nature spirits in communicating effectively with your animal.

They want to help, but can't unless you ask them.

4

Behavior & Training

Animal Misbehavior & How to Handle It

THERE IS AN INCREASING TREND TOWARDS 'NATURAL' animal care and training that reflects a shift to gentler methods after many years of viewing animals as automatons to be programmed to do our bidding, often through force. A new paradigm is evolving that acknowledges our connection to all things, living and nonliving, and demands respect and empathy for them.

If you adopt this point of view and learn to look at things through your animal's eyes, you will find you have greater success with respect to the behavior and training of your animal companion. The fundamental belief of this new outlook is that animals *ALWAYS* are doing what they believe to be appropriate, given the circumstances.

So if Fido is eating your couch, digging your garden or howling all night, he isn't bad. He is responding in the best way he knows how to whatever the situation is.

Your horse's inability to turn easily to one side or her fear of puddles of water aren't stubbornness or stupidity. Her instincts and perceptions help keep her alive and dictate her responses in a given situation.

Your cat may be soiling your rug rather than using the litter box, but he doesn't see it the way you do.

As frustrating as these behaviors can be, they are messages from your animal that need to be understood, not punished, because punishment does not treat the cause of the problem.

YOUR REACTION to Your Animal Friend

Behavior is an animal's way of communicating with us. Animals don't use language in the verbal sense, so they are restricted to 'acting out' what they want to tell us. Sometimes they bark or growl to tell us. Other times they paw at us or make motions with their bodies. A wagging or flicking tail, ears in various positions, and lips and teeth covered or not can communicate a great deal to us, just as they do to other animals.

Most people understand about these types of body language, which have been accepted and demonstrated by science, but they do not generalize and include all animal behavior in the category of communication. To become more effective and intuitive in dealing with your animal's behavior, you need to first learn to see things the way your animal sees them.

This is challenging for a number of reasons. Your first reaction to damaged possessions, soiled rugs or loud animal noises is likely to be highly emotional. The behavior triggers your anxiety about money, your concern about the neighbors complaining about your pet, or irritation at being disturbed.

If you react emotionally to your animal's message, then you won't be able to decode it. You will more than likely punish the animal for interrupting your work, play or sleep, or for damaging your belongings, without ever asking why he or she did it.

How often has this scenario played out in your relationship with your animals? Too often, probably. You are not alone in this. In a later section we will talk about why certain animals come into our lives, but suffice it to say that your emotional reaction is actually a sign that you need to work on yourself.

If you have tremendous stress or fears around money, neighbors, etc., you are not balanced energetically. You may well have issues whose buttons are being pushed by your animal's behavior. Look to yourself and evaluate your need for release of negative emotions, beliefs and fears. It is beyond the scope of this book to address this topic in depth, but it is worth pursuing if it seems appropriate.

DECODING **Animal Behavior**

Meanwhile, postpone an emotional reaction or punishment until you check out all the circumstances that created the situation. Your inclination is going to be to interpret your animal's actions based on human values, culture and prejudice.

Although domesticated animals fit rather well into our lives, that doesn't mean they share our values or perspective. If your dog, cat or horse refuses to do what is asked, there is a reason. You may consider it a good reason or a bad reason, but to them it is always a good reason.

Your challenge is to think as they do, feel as they do, and discover what their good reason is. Then you have to modify your behavior and expectations and training to get the desired results.

Sound complicated? It is. Humans are supposed to be smarter than animals, but inherent laziness prevents many people from using their 'smarts'.

How can you know how your animal feels and thinks? One way is to study the natural behavior patterns of the species of animal you have. For example, you may discover that beagles were bred to give voice on the hunt. Therefore, it is humans who are dumb to want them to stay silent.

Many useful facts can be gained through using your rational mind and studying the subject of behavior. Science has excelled in this type of work and revealed many basic behaviors of our companion animals.

The other way you can learn is through the use of your intuitive senses. Doing this is challenging, because it is impossible to give you a blueprint of what to do. When you assume your animal was 'right' in doing what he did, no matter how awful the results, and when you have a pretty good idea what is normal behavior for your animal, then you can begin to look at things through his eyes.

Animals are far less complex than humans. They have basic needs of food and shelter. They also need love. They have territorial and sexual habits that come from these basic needs, as well as behaviors that in nature allow them to get food, shelter and a mate and to care for and protect their young. They have tremendous energy levels that are required in nature, but usually are detrimental in the sedentary life they share with humans. Because they are empathetic creatures, they can absorb the negative energies you have. Your stresses, anxieties and fears all pile up in your animal companion.

In domesticating animals, we have taken away their ability to find their own food and take care of themselves. Now they are dependents and must rely on us for food, health care and love.

These variables can contribute to bad behavior and ill health in our pets, since we rely on the media and custom to dictate how we provide and care for our animals without finding out how healthful and effective these practices are.

. . .

STORIES OF MISBEHAVIOR

This section will consist of true stories about animals we have known. You will have the chance to think how you would have reacted in these circumstances, and hopefully learn to see things in a different way as a result of what we tell you.

ZIGGY THE NAUGHTY **Horse**

Ziggy was my young Lipizzan gelding. Every time Ziggy was approached with his bridle before a ride, he lifted his head dramatically away from it, making it a real nuisance to get it on him. Ziggy was a fairly green horse. He hadn't been trained or ridden much, and he clearly was intelligent and had a mind of his own. I was an equally green horse owner, and knew that horses, like many animals, will take advantage if given the chance.

Ziggy liked going for rides, or so I thought. But he didn't like getting tacked up. He was a bit better about his saddle, but seemed to tolerate rather than like it. Every time we went for a ride, it was the same. I had to struggle to get his bridle on and the bit in his mouth.

Once I finally succeeded, all was well. I noticed that he never seemed to mind taking it off. I learned from Pat Parelli's tapes how to teach Ziggy to drop his head. He liked natural horsemanship, and did very well with what I taught him. However, he resisted the bridle strongly despite all my efforts.

There were occasions when I wasn't feeling particularly patient, and I would speak harshly to him. The fact that he relented as soon as I yelled seemed to prove he was just being stubborn, so I went on thinking he was being a smart aleck.

I have seen people hit a horse for such obstinacy. In fact, the man who owned the boarding stables told me Ziggy was just being stubborn, and this man was supposedly an expert.

Ziggy had regular veterinary care, and the vet had floated his teeth and pronounced them free of problems. Most sources will advise you to have your animal checked for physical problems before assuming that his behavior is due to stubbornness.

What I didn't realize was that veterinarians frequently have not been thoroughly schooled in equine dental problems. When I became acquainted with the practice of equine dentistry as a specialty, I made an appointment. The specialist came out with a vet and checked Ziggy. It required anesthesia and an assistant. Ziggy's mouth was propped open with a special tool and examined far more closely than the vet had been able to. There were many things wrong with his teeth, but they were all fixable.

After the dentist did his work, Ziggy never again pulled away when I went to put on his bridle. I had great feelings of guilt for having been judgmental towards him.

Would you have made a similar mistake?

How Often Does This Happen?

Fear is a common obstacle to deal with in training, especially animals like horses, which are prey animals, not predators. They tend to have more fearful temperaments than predatory species like dogs and cats.

Before I owned my own horse, I would rent horses to ride. We tried several places. One was out in North Phoenix in the desert with a self-professed retired cowboy.

He had a pretty mare he said he got from the Indian reservation. She seemed a bit timid, but willing. He wanted her to jump over a railroad tie, and she resisted, so he whipped her with his riding crop. After multiple hits, she went over the tie. Then he decided she had to do it again. (He was lucky I didn't have a gun.) He began to whip her again, because she refused, and finally she did as he asked.

He mounted her and came over to where we were and said he knew I was upset by what he did, but that `a horse isn't worth a damn if it can't take a beating'. I told him what I thought, and we never went back there.

TAMMI THE NAUGHTY *Akita*

Tammi was my Akita. The breed is known for being aloof and loyal, but also can be aggressive towards other dogs or children, depending on breeding. I had made a point with the breeder that I wanted a dog with excellent temperament, especially towards children, so you can imagine how dismayed I was to see that Tammi went from being a sweet puppy around children to an adult that had little patience with their antics.

I was concerned about what harm she might do. Although she wasn't aggressive, she would often turn her open mouth towards children if they closed in around her head too quickly. She never bit, but she did hit one child with a canine tooth, creating a small puncture wound. Fortunately, the parents were tolerant, realizing their child had pushed her a bit. I remember the second time she did this was to my niece. I was so embarrassed and frightened for my niece (the small wound was right near her eye) that I smacked Tammi on the face and fussed at her.

I will never forget her obvious surprise, as I almost never had hit her in ten years. She clearly didn't understand why I would do that. I knew at that moment that she hadn't acted out of bad temper, and that she had felt justified, and in fact was hurt that I had reacted as I did.

I had recently begun dowsing (see the `Dowsing to Help Animals' section for more details on this technique), and I used dowsing to discover that Tammi had some dental issues.

We took her to a specialist in Scottsdale, who found that in addition to some common problems older dogs have, such as a tooth that required pulling, she had an abscess in her canine tooth that was the biggest he had ever seen.(This specialist did dental work on the big cats at the Phoenix zoo.) Indeed, he said she had probably had it most of her life, and it had been causing her pain; a lot of pain. The tooth had been broken when she was a puppy trying to eat her way out of her crate. My vet at the time had assured me there was no need to worry about it. Unfortunately, he was wrong, and it is hard to imagine the pain she had suffered for almost nine years.

Looking back, I could see that her change in behavior towards children coincided with that abscess. After $1400 worth of dental care, which included a gold crown on the canine, Tammi became a different animal. She was great with my niece, and in fact became good friends with her. Her general attitude was more mellow and relaxed.

It was clear her behavior had been pain-related, and in fact, she had shown restraint in her response to children messing with her face. If I hadn't become a dowser, it never would have occurred to me to check that out. I accepted what the vet said about her tooth, and I adopted the current attitudes about Akitas and passed judgment on her wrongly.

How would you have acted in my shoes?

How to React Appropriately to Animal Misbehavior

The previous two examples are meant to help you see how easy it is to misinterpret animal behavior. What is at fault?

The first problem is when you don't assume your animal was doing its best at the time. If you react judgmentally or emotionally, you will most likely make a mistake.

Secondly, if you accept whatever the current negative thought is about your type of animal, whether it is a breed characteristic, as with my Akita, or a general aphorism about animals in general, as with my horse, you set yourself up for misinterpretations, because you aren't looking at things from your animal's perspective.

Third, don't always accept 'expert' advice. Listen to your intuition. Vets aren't always animal behavior specialists, and they don't always have a lot of training in various specialties such as dentistry and nutrition. Someone who has had horses or dogs for years is not necessarily an expert. Seek a second opinion if you feel it is needed.

Most importantly, empower yourself by learning an intuitive technique such as dowsing.

Sometimes it is difficult to solve a clash in behaviors. Our dogs are 'rescue dogs', adopted from the Humane Society or off the street. Since they were young dogs at liberty in the Sonoran desert near Phoenix, they had encounters with coyotes. Both dogs were under 20 pounds and malnourished when we adopted them and would have been good prey for hungry coyotes. Roger used to shiver whenever he heard coyotes howl, but later he started barking an alarm. India was less prone to bark, but did on occasion when she heard a pack nearby. They did this to let us know something dangerous was nearby. They knew that was their job.

We have told them countless times that the coyotes can't harm us inside the house, but they seem to doubt what we say. So they continued to wake us at night barking in response to howling coyotes.

In part, their response was also probably territorial in nature. It is extremely difficult to change behaviors that are adapted for basic survival needs, but in a later section we will discuss some energetic techniques that may help in this type of circumstance.

DISCOVER the Real Roots of Animal Misbehavior

It is a challenge to change your viewpoint from conventional to more natural. But there are a number of reasons to do so. You will enhance your own health if you forgo judgment and emotional reactions such as anger and rage. They do nothing to change what has happened or your animal's behavior, and they can weaken the bond of trust you have with her.

By approaching an incident of apparent 'misbehavior' first and foremost from the animal's point of view, you have the opportunity to see that in her eyes, she wasn't doing wrong at all. If you practice the communication techniques described in an earlier chapter, you will be more likely to find out her reasons for what she did.

On many occasions, you will discover fear, pain or anxiety at the root of the behavior. Unless you treat these, the behavior will either continue or morph into something worse. By finding out the root cause of the behavior, you can then work at a proper resolution of your animal's problem, whether it be physical, emotional or energetic. We discuss many options in a later section.

This all may sound great in theory, but it is challenging in practice, as it requires you to change basic behavior patterns of your own in order to change those of your animal. It is a good lesson. If you find it so difficult to change yourself, you might have some sympathy for your poor animal. After all, we are supposed to be the smarter ones.

To Train or Not?

Training is a way of communicating with your animal companion. It lets your animal know what you desire when you say or do certain things. It establishes boundaries of acceptable behavior. It helps you to spend constructive time bonding with your animal.

Training is an excellent way of asserting your dominance in the relationship, by showing you are the teacher and your animal is the student (although the reality is a bit more complicated). Most fundamentally, training allows you to connect with your animal.

There are countless methods of training dogs, horses and other species. Some of them work, some don't, and some work really well. It is beyond the scope of this book to cover this subject in depth, but we will present you with some items for your consideration so that you can choose the program that will work best for you.

Each animal is an individual, as is each human. You must seek out the training technique that resonates with you and appeals to your animal if you want to have optimal results.

How to Make a Decision about Training

In general, regardless of species, there are some things to consider before you begin a training program with your animal: Make sure your animal is in excellent physical condition. You may elect to have him checked by a vet or other professional to determine he is physically capable of the program you want to embark on. This is especially true of horses, who due to poor nutrition and lack of exercise are frequently not really fit for the athletic training programs people desire them to participate in.

Read, study, research the internet or ask about the various programs that seem good to you. Check cost, duration, location and qualifications of teachers. Examine the methods used in the program. If there is any pain involved, find another program. Your animal should enjoy the classes in order to learn the most he or she can.

If you are sending your animal away for training, it is very important that you be assured that your animal will be treated with respect and fed and housed according your instructions, as appropriate. For example, the culture of training horses seems to involve the trainer deciding a lot more than training issues. This is not always in the best interest of your horse, as most trainers are not experts in all aspects of horse care.

Be sure you have set boundaries you can live with before you commit to a program. We have seen and heard of horse trainers changing diet and treating horses for physical issues without consulting the owners. If you are content with this, that will work fine. If you have your own program, it may create problems. The same is true for any training program where you board any type of animal. Get everything in writing and set appropriate boundaries before you drop your animal off.

Roll Over, Horse!: An Example of Natural Training

My horse Ziggy was a Lipizzan, the dancing breed of white horses from Austria. I always thought they were absolutely beautiful.

Before I became involved in dowsing and animal communication, I got Ziggy and began working with him. We decided to board him for two weeks of intensive training in Scottsdale at a dressage facility. We went over daily for lessons and to visit our horses.

Ziggy made dismal progress, resisting what he was being taught. As I rode him during the lessons, I could feel he didn't want to be doing dressage. I did not pursue further training of that sort after the two weeks was up. I had learned an expensive lesson.

Instead, we began natural horsemanship training through Pat Parelli. Ziggy showed a real talent for that type of work, and seemed to enjoy it thoroughly. He learned many things with few tries, and it gave us a great opportunity to bond as we improved how we interacted.

Sometimes you can train your animal without formal classes, as long as you choose something they want to learn and are a patient teacher. I noticed that Ziggy liked to roll in the sand of the round pen after a bath, so I decided to teach him to lie down and roll over on command. Since he liked carrots so much, and since I was merely teaching a variation of something he already did, it was relatively easy.

People could hardly believe when I would show them how he would let me slip onto his bare back from the fence and tell him to go lie down. I would then get off and tell him to roll over, which he did. He also did it on command if I was standing next to him. This worked because it played to both of our strengths. Learn your strengths and those of your animal, and you can have wonderful results, too.

TRAINING SHOULD BE FUN!

Choose a training method that as closely as possible mimics the natural behavior of your animal and administers corrections humanely and in a way that the animal will understand easily. See what rewards are used, whether love, treats or a toy.

Look at what the goals of the program are. Do they match your own? Are they realistic? Will they enhance the health and/or happiness of your animal? Suitable goals include, but are not limited to, teaching your animal a job, giving him a chance to exercise and work off energy, or helping him develop a natural talent.

You might enter a program that has competition as its focus, such as agility, obedience or dressage. Make sure your animal wants to compete, and that you are capable of making competition fun, or you will only be adding stress to your animal's life.

Talk to your animal, or have an animal communicator talk to him. Does your animal like the idea of the class? As with children, perhaps he doesn't, but will grow to like it. As long as fear is not an issue, you can start a class and check with your animal after a while and see how he likes it. If he still doesn't like it, you need to re-evaluate it, because you may just be wasting time and money.

If you have to send your animal away for training, make sure he or she understands what is going on, and has no objection to being away from you, or problems may result.

Once you have gone to some classes, re-evaluate the program. Make sure you are both happy with it and that you are seeing progress. Don't throw good time and money after bad.

Caring For Your Animal Companion

53

If you are stressed and angry during the training session, quit that program. If you can't find a program that doesn't stress you or make you emotional, seriously consider getting some energetic clearing on yourself. Don't focus your negative reactions on your animal. Remember, training is supposed to be positive for both of you. If you aren't having some fun, something is wrong.

SUMMARY

1. Your animal's behavior is neither good nor bad. Each animal is doing the best he can in any given situation.

2. You are the one who judges behavior as good or bad based on personal and cultural prejudices, and those criteria mean absolutely nothing to your animal. Therefore, when you judge your animal, you are widening the gap between you, a gap that is already present in all interspecies relationships.

3. Your judgment of your animal as being 'bad', and your emotional response to such behavior does nothing to erase the behavior or its cause. It merely heaps more stress on your animal, erodes trust, creates misunderstanding and harms your own physical health.

4. Training is a method of communicating your desires to your animal. It is also a great way to bond. It also can create behaviors that enhance your relationship.

5. Training should have a strong element of fun for both you and your animal. It should never involve pain or stress. Choose a program that resonates with you, gives you satisfaction and enhances your relationship with your animal.

6. Don't train your animal for competition unless you are certain your animal is comfortable with competition, and you aren't going to be stressed out by losing. Your stress will be communicated to your animal and potentially harm its health. It is also counterproductive to any elective activity to have undue stress be a part of it.

7. Before embarking on any training program, make sure your animal and you are both completely fit physically for it. Many animals have physical challenges that don't show up in a sedentary existence, but create pain and difficulty if they enter a training regimen. Other times, the animal is simply not in condition to perform what he or she is being asked to do.

8. If you believe your animal has abnormal fear or stress in the presence of other animals, during travel, in new situations, or during training sessions, consider professional help to clear any energetic issues that may be contributing to this.

5

Emotions & How To Deal With Them

Emotions: The Heart of the Matter

SCIENCE HASN'T ADDRESSED the subject of animal emotions. Emotions are hard enough to explain or verify in humans, let alone animals. Yet we know beyond a shadow of a doubt that we *FEEL*.

Many people are likewise convinced that their animal friends have feelings. Most pet owners can relate experiences that they believe represent feelings of love, anger or sadness in their animals. Just about anyone believes that animals can feel fear or anxiety.

Emotions are powerful. Metaphysically, they provide the fuel for creating your life experiences. Most of the world's religions believe in the power of love and preach that we are better off if we release hate and fear through forgiveness and tolerance.

If you study metaphysics, you learn that the emotional energies you hold are the ones that attract your experiences. Like attracts like, and therefore, birds of a feather do flock together. Mistrust and paranoia attract situations that engender more mistrust and paranoia. Hatred begets hatred. Therefore it is critical that negative emotions be released if you are to create a happy and healthy life for yourself.

This isn't that far-fetched. Science has indeed demonstrated that certain personalities are more likely to have heart attacks, and it isn't the loving, easy-going ones. Research has shown that you will live a longer, happier life if you aren't lonely and if you have a purpose to your life. People who have pets seem to live longer than those without.

You could conclude that reducing unnecessary stress, having a sense of purpose and connecting with other living things, both human and animal, will help you live longer and be healthier. So Science in a sense is validating what many religions have said for eons, albeit in a slightly different way.

What Do Animals Feel?

For the purposes of this section we will assume that animals do indeed have emotions. They may be pictured as less complex than humans, but just as powerful.

Fear, love, anxiety and anger appear to be just as powerful in animals as they are in humans. Animals can be phobic just as humans can.

There are wonderful tales of animals helping their humans, and although one can't prove they are doing it for love, neither could you prove humans do anything for purely altruistic reasons.

Separation anxiety is recognized in many companion animals as the major cause of misbehavior when left alone. Anger is less explored, but is an equally powerful emotion in the animal world. We believe anger is the root of many behavioral issues in animals. It is merely suppressed, because it is considered unacceptable by humans. It is fairly common in abused, neglected or rescue animals.

By accepting the idea that your animal can have basic feelings like you, you will be better able to understand and connect with her. Make an effort to be aware of your animal's feelings.

This doesn't mean you should think how *YOU* would feel in her shoes. Become conscious of how *SHE* feels in her shoes. This must not be used as an excuse to judge your animal. Some people who don't even believe animals have emotions will attribute guilty feelings to them in some situations. What is interpreted as guilt in some cases may well be, but many times it is merely the anticipation of the human's displeasure.

FOLLOW **Nature to Keep Emotions Balanced**

Learning about the normal behavior pattern, requirements and energy level of your animal will help in this endeavor. If you understand the basic needs of your animal and how they are met in nature, and if you understand the normal level of activity of your animal, as well as the social life of its species, you will have a far better idea of how it feels living with you.

For example, most animals in the wild have rather large home territories or ranges. Yet we confine our companion animals to small stalls, crates, yards and rooms. Is it any wonder they develop behaviors that are unwanted due to the stress of confinement?

The energy level of most living things is high enough to allow them to forage for food, defend themselves from predators, find and attract a mate and raise a family under very challenging conditions. Yet we fail to give most of our animals an outlet for this energy and are surprised when they eat the couch, dig up the yard or become cribbers. Instead, humans are indignant that pets who are 'given everything' can react so 'badly'. (We hear the same thing from some parents about their children.)

Almost all animals are social to some degree. Horses live in herds. Wild dogs live in packs. Even cats in the wild form attachments and raise families. How many people get just one animal as a pet or companion and then leave it at home alone or alone at a boarding facility for long periods of time? Loneliness can lead to stress and misbehavior.

Without proper socialization, an animal can develop problems interacting with its own kind, or even with other humans. This can be particularly problematic when dogs behave badly towards children because they have not been properly socialized with them.

Eating is a social occasion for many animals, as it should be for humans. Given the opportunity, your animal friend may prefer to eat when you or his animal friends are eating, not all by himself. Digestive problems and eating disorders can potentially stem from the stress of 'unnatural' eating patterns.

By taking the time to learn about your animal's natural needs and preferences, you can create a living situation that will reduce negative emotions such as fear, anxiety, stress and anger. This will require time and research on your part, but it will be worth your effort.

The next section will address how to handle negative emotions that are currently affecting your animal friend.

Clearing Negative Emotions

If you are getting a new animal companion, you can research about it and follow the suggestions of the previous sections, but what about an animal that you already have who has problems? Or the adult animal you acquire? Is there anything that can be done to help them? The answer is yes.

It is possible to make changes in your animal's behavior and emotional condition, but it is much simpler not to allow problems to develop in the first place. So be aware at the outset that it will be a project to help your pet become better adapted and problem free if he or she has current 'issues'.

It will require a commitment of time, effort and probably money to effect the change you wish to see. However, it will be well worth your effort and will save you heartache and money in the long run, as well as give you far better relationship with your animal.

Why Clear Negative Emotions?

For the purposes of this section, we will discuss rescue animals and how important it is to clear negative emotions from them, as well as ways this can be done. (All animals benefit from clearing negative energies, but it is more evident in rescue animals.)

A rescue animal will be defined as one who comes from an animal shelter, or is 'found' wandering at large, or comes from obvious circumstances of neglect and/or abuse. You may also consider an animal who has been passed from owner to owner as a rescue.

Rescuing is the most challenging situation as a rule for establishing a happy, healthy and emotionally whole relationship with an animal. While it is admirable to acquire your animals from such conditions, it is important to be aware of the special needs of such animals.

All of our companion animals are rescue animals, and because we have the tools needed to help them adjust to living with humans, we have had excellent results. Our animals are now healthy, well-adjusted and happy, though they weren't when we got them.

The older or more abused the animal, the bigger the job is. Why is that? Just like humans, animals attract or create situations in their environment that resonate with the energies they are holding.

Most people have known a fearful human or animal that seemed to attract attack very easily. By holding a lot of energy that could be called 'fear of attack', a person or animal magnetizes such events. The more times they are attacked, the more energy they hold, and it becomes a downward spiral.

Fear is a potent emotional energy in animals, and comes in many flavors, such as fear of abandonment, fear of punishment and fear of attack. The more of this negative energy they hold, the harder it is for them to behave normally.

Helping a Cat Mellow Out

Spike was an older male cat who had a tendency to bite his owner with very little provocation. His human came to us and asked if we could help stop the biting, as he had hurt her pretty badly, drawing blood. Sometimes the attacks came at night while she slept, and she was fearful of them.

A clearing revealed that Spike had many negative energies that would predispose him to biting, with 'bite' being one of the most prevalent. After two clearings and some pulsed magnetic therapy treatments, Spike became far more placid. He even stayed in the room when we went to visit, although in the past he had run away from us. His full treatment lasted months, but it saved his life. It certainly saved his relationship with his human, who was thrilled with the change in him.

The Wired Australian Shepherd

Our dog India came to us as a malnourished 17-pound dog who was basically three-legged. She had been hit by a car and her hip was broken. She had surgery to repair the damage, as well as having been spayed, and she had a lot of physical and emotional challenges. However, she was the cutest and sweetest girl, and we knew she was meant to be ours and that she would become whole if given the chance.

At the time we were using Spiritual Response Therapy (SRT), and in addition to good nutrition and healing sessions with Reiki and Spiritual Healing, we did SRT on her many times.

We could tell when she needed a treatment, as her eyes would get wide, showing the whites, and she would become hyperactive and 'bounce off the walls'. She had a lot of negative energies to detox, but over time, she became calm around motor vehicles, stopped throwing up in the car, and became very calm and easy to handle.

She also no longer had a desire to chew things when we left her at home. She became a 50-pound, thickly furred, bright-eyed and responsible dog who was the apple of Nigel's eye. There is no doubt in our minds that without the clearing work, she would still have certain behavioral challenges due to negative energies.

Based on our experience, we believe animals that have been bred to work closely with humans, the way sheepdogs do, often are more sensitive to human energies and have a tendency to absorb and then reflect those energies. Dogs in general seem to absorb noxious energies, sometimes on purpose as a way of protecting their humans. Since energies that harm humans are also noxious for dogs, this leads to health problems. Knowing a method that clears negative energies is very helpful in supporting your animal's health and well-being.

A later section deals with the physical health problems of rescue animals. In this discussion we will only address the emotional needs of such animals. When working with emotions, it is not adequate to treat the animal's physical body only.

Animals are very in tune with energy, and they respond well to what is called 'vibrational medicine', or treatments that are aimed at the energetic portion of the body, sometimes called the subtle energy body. Included in this category are various healing techniques such as Reiki, Spiritual Response Therapy, EFT (Emotional Freedom Technique) and energy clearing, plus products that affect the subtle energy body, such as flower essences and aromatherapy.

The energy body is where negative emotions lurk, and energy therapies target them more effectively in most cases than physical modalities, though there are some exceptions. It is beyond the scope of this book to teach you how to use these techniques and products, but you can search the internet for more information on these subjects.

At this time, we will make suggestions for using these energetic modalities to help clear your animal of negative emotions.

Use a Variety of Approaches

Work on proper nutrition for your animal. Feeding his physical body the best possible food will aid in the healing and detoxification process.

Spend lots of time communicating your love and your goals to your animal, and finding out what his are. Commune with your animal and become accustomed to how he expresses his feelings of fear and love. Take the time to learn his language.

When you are certain your animal has become physically fit and used to your relationship, consider a good training program that will allow you to bond further with your animal and help him understand what you desire in the relationship. These will all help your animal adjust to becoming a member of your family.

However, how do you get rid of negative energies that came from previous experiences? This is when energy work comes into play.

While there are many effective methods, we will mention the ones we ourselves have used with good results. We now use our own approach to balance the energies internally and externally for animals and humans. On the way to developing our own approach, we used many different energy modalities. They all had strengths and weaknesses. They are mentioned below, as they gave us much useful experience and helped us to create our own unique approach that we believe will treat any problem situation.

We have found that there are many different energy clearing techniques available. Some identify and then clear each negative belief, some just work on clearing energies blocking the situation. It used to be a difficult thing to find such practitioners, but now the concept is more widely accepted and there are many more opportunities to learn for yourself or to find practitioners you resonate with.

One tool we have used with success in the past is Spiritual Response Therapy. This system is practiced by qualified practitioners and uses dowsing to identify and clear energetic problems.

Other energetic techniques that provide useful support when there are negative emotions are Reiki and Spiritual Healing. We find these methods useful, but not as powerful at identifying and transforming the negative energies quickly in most cases.

The easiest way to discover whether you feel a method is for you is to have a treatment from a professional first. Then decide if you wish to pursue a course of study in that method, or perhaps find another you like better.

Don't assume that the negative events in your animal's past have to be ignored, or even *CAN* be ignored. Whatever they are, and whether you know what they are or not, they are affecting your animal's behavior and happiness. By helping clear your animal of such influences, you will have a happier relationship, and your animal will be healthier.

There are products on the market that work at the energetic level to release fear and other negative emotions. Bach Rescue Remedy is a flower essence that is perhaps the most well-known treatment for animals who are stressed in any way. There are other brands that address modern issues more effectively than the Bach brand, in our opinion, but Rescue Remedy is a good, all-purpose emergency remedy that we keep on hand.

We work with the Australian Bush Flower Essences, dowsing custom combinations that address the specific challenges and have found them to be very effective and free of side effects.

Homeopathics are another type of subtle energy medicine that can help heal emotional energies. Unless you are a Master Dowser specializing in health, we suggest you work with a professional homeopath for best results with this modality.

Because many animals have an acute sense of smell, aromatherapy has great possibilities for helping to gently make changes. Consult with an experienced practitioner or get a good course of study for best results. Fragrances have been shown scientifically to produce results even in humans.

Whatever program of therapy you undertake, be patient and realize that it may take time to see results. For rescue animals, it can easily take one to two years for complete physical and emotional healing.

Don't quit working on your animal just because the worst behaviors have ceased. Continue to do clearing work regularly on your pet to maintain the optimum level of health and performance.

6

Physical Health

Help Your Animal to Better Health

WHAT IS GOOD HEALTH? Is good health merely the absence of pain?

Most people avoid thinking about their animal's health until he or she is in obvious pain. We encourage you to develop a new attitude about health as relates to your animal friend. Don't wait until your animal develops a dreadful symptom before you think about the subject of health. If you have that attitude, you are saying you can't help your animal be healthy. Only a professional can do that, and then only *AFTER* health has gone. Perhaps you actually believe that, but it is time to consider another viewpoint.

Consider the possibility that optimal health is something you create by doing certain things, and that you have a LOT of control over these things. Good health means having a lot of energy or vitality. A healthy animal also has a strong immune system, and doesn't have lots of allergies or infectious diseases.

You can tell a healthy animal by its coat, which is thick, soft and lustrous. A healthy animal has bright, clear eyes. A smooth, flowing gait and well-muscled body are also signs of optimal health. If your animal companion is overweight, has skin conditions, or lacks energy, then she isn't as healthy as she could be.

Notice that we don't suggest that taking your dog in for a yearly exam and shots is an adequate health program. This type of program parallels the human annual checkup, and while it may catch certain conditions before they progress, it does not proactively create optimal health. That requires more effort. This section will introduce you to many practical things you can do to help your animal achieve optimal health.

It has been our observation that people who care about their own health and actively work to improve it usually are more open to helping their animals achieve perfect health. Humans who have no concern for maintaining their own health frequently are unwilling to take the time and effort to help their animal companions achieve good health. So by taking the time to work on your animal's health, you may discover you change your attitude about your own health program.

The suggestions we make in this section largely rely on providing what Nature intended the physical body to have for optimal health, or at least offering the best substitute available. In discovering what these things are, you will be engaging your intuition as well as your practical side.

What to Feed?

What you feed your animal is perhaps the single most important factor in creating good health. It cannot be overemphasized how much diet affects health. You have probably heard the expression 'you are what you eat'. This is as true in animals as it is in humans.

. . .

WATER

Let's look first at what your animal drinks. Water makes up most of the physical body. If you give your animal water that isn't healthy, then that will compromise your animal's health.

Look at the source of water you use for your pet. Tap water contains many chemicals to kill bacteria and other detrimental organisms. It can also be contaminated with harmful chemicals. Although minimum levels are set for many chemicals, there are some who question how safe those levels are in the long term.

We have seen animals who won't drink tap water unless they are very, very thirsty. Most animals, especially cats, show a natural preference for flowing water, which is a reflection on the vitality of it. Given a choice, most animals will choose to drink filtered or spring water over tap water.

In other words, even though they aren't wild animals, they know what kind of water Mother Nature intended them to drink. Most humans are not that discriminating, though the disdain most humans have for drinking water may well stem from having tap water as the main source of this vital element.

We strongly urge you to make sure your animal has water that is free of chemicals, whether it is filtered, distilled, reverse osmosis or spring water. It is not expensive to fit your tap with a filtering system or to get a filter pitcher, and it will improve the quality of your water tremendously. Reverse osmosis systems can be purchased for a reasonable price at places such as Costco and Home Depot, but bear in mind they require periodic maintenance.

FOOD FOR DOGS and Cats

The type of food you feed is the other important part of a proper, healthy diet. By becoming aware of the role of diet in your animal's health, you can also become more healthy yourself. In order to maintain optimal health, your animal's body needs good fuel. Not only the right amount of calories per day, but the building blocks for growth, repair and maintenance. These calories and building blocks are present in your animal's food.

How can you tell if the food is high quality? Find out what your animal would eat in the wild. The best feeds provide the nutrition that a natural diet would. For cats and dogs, a raw food diet that mimics optimal food in the wild is best, but although there are many books and resources on this subject, most people find it too challenging to provide a well-balanced raw food diet for their pets. We suggest that if you do feed this diet, that you supplement it to overcome any nutritional lacks due to our food sources being of poor nutritional quality, whether organic or not.

Let me repeat that: there are not enough minerals and vitamins in our food these days, so unless you have your own organic garden, and you feed the soil (not just fertilizers), then you *MUST* supplement for optimal health.

The next best way to feed your dog or cat is to use a naturally-preserved or preservative-free feed that has the best quality protein sources and the proper balance of various other elements such as fats. Some of the better brands add nutrients such as vitamins and minerals or herbs and enzymes. These additives will be discussed in the Why Supplement? section.

Most of the best brands of food cannot be found in grocery stores, as they have too short a shelf life. They either have to be special-ordered or ordered from a dealer, or bought at a boutique-type pet shop or grooming parlor that specializes in natural foods. This ensures maximum freshness.

Foods purchased in grocery stores often have questionable preservatives such as ethoxyquin, which is a rubber stabilizer used to keep the fats from going rancid in the foods. Obviously, it would be better to eat the food before the fats go rancid.

Dogs and cats benefit from having green foods. Cats usually love to chew fresh grass, and if you don't have natural untreated lawn at home, you can buy little kits at the pet store to grow a small flat of grass for your cats. Alternatively, dogs and cats both seem to enjoy having well-chopped, steamed organic green veggies mixed with their food daily (less for cats than for dogs). The fresh greens and fiber will not only provide nutrients, but probably will help scour out the digestive tract, reducing hairballs. It is also possible to buy green supplements, but they lack some of the fine ingredients of fresh greens.

Don't forget that cats need moist food as a major component of their diet. Urinary tract issues can ensue when a totally dry food diet is adhered to for long periods of time, especially in male cats, and if the food is not the highest quality. There are a number of good brands of high quality canned cat food available, but most are NOT in the grocery store. Pet boutiques and health food stores often have these brands. However, we have noticed that as consumers demand higher quality pet foods, the stores are finding ways to provide them.

Many of the newer brands of dry kibble for dogs and cats are now grain-free. A large number of animals are allergic or sensitive to grains. In most cases, grains are just used for filler, not because the animal would seek them out in the wild. Consider trying a grain-free formula for your pet, even if you see no signs of allergies. We have had great results.

Try to avoid any foods that contain a lot of things your animal would not choose to eat in the wild. Some grain-free foods are now substituting starchy veggies like sweet potatoes. It's a cost-cutting thing.

Another thing to watch for is protein content. While in the old days, poor quality foods had low protein levels, we are beginning to see on rare occasions, high end pet foods with what we feel is too MUCH protein. Educate yourself on the appropriate amount of protein for your species of animal, and make sure the feed matches his or her requirements, but doesn't overdo. Too much protein is as bad as too little, especially in sedentary animals.

Where the protein comes from is also important. Educate yourself on the sources of protein in pet foods. Choose the highest quality you can afford.

Horses and Small Herbivores (Like Rabbits)

If your animal friend is a herbivore such as a horse or a rabbit, he has different nutritional requirements than a cat or dog. Animals that eat exclusively plant matter are called 'herbivores'. The type of plants they eat in nature may not be available to you, so you will need to design a program that gives them as close to a natural diet as possible.

Alfalfa is commonly used for horses and rabbits. The protein content of alfalfa is too high for these animals in most cases. Grass hay is usually healthier for companion herbivores, and is less likely to upset the digestive system of the animal. Orchard grass or timothy fall into this category.

Herbivores have sensitive digestive systems and are prone to a condition called colic. Proper nutrition, water and exercise will eliminate colic in many cases. Since colic is a deadly condition in horses, we cannot overemphasize this point.

Hay of all sorts can be treated with chemicals. Animals can be sensitive to such chemicals, so if you can get a 'clean' source of hay, your animal will be better off. Select hay that has good green color.

Straw, like hay, only gives fiber and is lacking in nutrients. Grain or pellets are used to supplement the diet of most companion herbivores. If you use a prepared brand of pellets, check the ingredients. Avoid anything with preservatives such as ethoxyquin and sugar or sweeteners such as molasses and beet pulp. These additives are present for commercial reasons, not nutritional ones. They prolong shelf life or make a poor formula more palatable, which increases the sales of the company selling the product.

Pellets ideally should be from sources which are not exposed to pesticides, though this is a challenge. Any additives should be of the highest quality and bioavailable, that is, easily assimilated into the body.

Don't overfeed grains, especially to sedentary animals. They can become fat, diabetic or allergic.

Because the digestive systems of herbivores are sensitive, digestive aids can be useful. In particular, pro- and pre-biotics are very useful. They can also be used at times of digestive stress. Digestive aids perform best when used regularly.

My rabbits responded well to replacing their water with peppermint or chamomile tea at room temperature when they had digestive upsets. After a few days on the tea, I switched back to pure water, and they always got better.

Being aware of when your animal is hurting is vital to catching such things before they require veterinary care. My rabbits always got very quiet and tense when they had digestive distress, which fortunately, was rare.

Moki was a miniature black bunny I got from a rescue organization. She had been abused and poorly fed (reportedly on Oreo cookies), and the director said she could not digest fresh vegetables, as they gave her diarrhea. The conventional wisdom said that she must stay on a strict diet of hay and pellets until she healed, but that could take months. I wondered how she could heal on a diet of that sort. Occasionally I would try her on veggies, only to have her develop loose stools.

I looked everywhere for a preservative-free rabbit chow, but couldn't find one. She refused to eat pellets, and my opinion was that she disliked the ethoxyquin. Finally, I discovered that the natural, organic pelleted grain ration which we had been using for our horses with excellent results, would work equally well for rabbits. So I tried her on some. She ate them with great gusto, and her health turned around quickly. With the added probiotic she was soon able to eat any fresh vegetables she liked, even organic lettuce.

GENERAL DIETARY GUIDELINES for All Animals

Whatever species of animal you have, try to feed it as close to a natural diet as possible. Avoid preservatives, chemicals and additives. Don't use sugar or sweet feeds. Be aware that many dealers of hay and feed makers use pesticides in their mills. Get the cleanest source of feed you can.

It isn't enough to read the label. Labels don't always list every ingredient or chemical that your feed has been exposed to. Even if a label says the ingredients are 'human quality' or 'human grade', that doesn't necessarily mean they are healthy. Human grade foods often have antibiotic, hormone and pesticide residues in them. Read labels carefully and ask questions. Visit the website of the company and speak to a representative. Be very cautious about using anything like treats from countries that do not have strict regulations. Check the country of origin and reject anything questionable. Price is an indication of quality in cases like this.

Finicky animals are not always just being difficult. Animals have very sensitive noses and palates. They are capable of detecting chemicals and rancidity that we couldn't detect. They are also more in tune with nature, so they tend to prefer clean, natural foods.

I remember the case of the German Shepherd dog whose family had gone on a trip and left her in the care of two different babysitters. One person visited the home in the morning, while the other person visited at night. The family was gone a week. When they returned, the dog had lost a significant amount of weight. On asking the caregivers, they discovered that each thought the other was feeding, as the dog's bowl was always full. The dog had only had treats and water all week, which explained her begging so much. The food, which was bought from a high-end company, had a problem with an ingredient that had turned bad. The owner could smell it in the food, and so could the dog, who refused to eat it. Even good quality food can have problems sometimes.

If you can't get your animal to switch to a healthier diet, make sure you do indeed have a healthier choice, and then make the transition slowly. Animals, like people, can become addicted to sweets and other additives that aren't good for them.

Mix the new food with the old in increasingly greater proportions over a period of time. With some animals, this can take a week, but with others, it may take months. Also bear in mind that energetically, an animal attracted to junk food, which has a low vibration, must himself be at a low vibration. Remember that like attracts like? (When you're feeling 'down', do you reach for something really healthy to eat or drink, or do you go for 'comfort food'?) Consider energy clearing work to raise his vibration for optimal health.

How Dowsing/Natural Knowing Can Help

Dowsing is helpful when deciding the best way to transition into another brand of food. Changing to a good brand too quickly may produce a detox reaction that actually looks like an illness or cold. The animal may vomit, have diarrhea or have cold symptoms. He could develop skin issues like itching, hives or oozing.

This is not pleasant for you or your pet, so make sure you take long enough to make the change so the body can release toxins more slowly. Detoxing will aid health, but it is more pleasant to do it slowly.

If you are a dowser, or if you are able to muscle test, you can find out what food is best for your animal using your Natural Knowing ability. You don't have to put your trust in what someone else says. Your intuition and your animal's body know what is best.

It is very worthwhile to learn to evaluate different types of feeds in this way, as well as educating yourself about what the best natural diet is.

The time, effort and money you put into buying a truly healthy feed for your animal will be repaid many times over. Your animal will live a longer, healthier life. You will have fewer degenerative diseases to cope with, and lower vet bills.

Why Supplement?

Why should you use nutritional supplements for your pet? Especially if you use a top quality food, is it really necessary?

This is a good question, and depends on a lot of factors. Nutritional supplementation is suggested when your animal is not getting all the nutrients he needs from his diet.

What are possible reasons for this? The main reason would be if the food you are feeding is not the best quality. Vitamins and minerals will be lacking in poor quality feeds, such as many that are sold in grocery or pet stores. If you choose to feed one of the cheaper brands, which we don't recommend, you can counter some of the poor quality by giving a good brand of supplement to provide vitamins and minerals that are lacking in the diet.

Even if you are feeding an all-natural, organic diet of the best foods possible, your animal may benefit from supplements, especially minerals. Our soils are being depleted of minerals, and even organically grown food is sometimes mineral-poor. Or the animal may have a deficiency due to physiological problems.

This is a situation where dowsing or muscle testing is a big help, because you can find out what he needs. Each animal is an individual, and even a perfect diet may be lacking in certain things to encourage optimal digestion and absorption.

Unless you are feeding raw, uncooked food, your animal's diet probably is low in enzymes, which are destroyed by heat and processing. Enzymes are required for proper digestion. Your carnivorous animal (dog or cat) will benefit from being given raw, organic meat bones to eat regularly. Not only is it good for the teeth, it will provide them with nutrients not available in processed foods. Don't cook the bones. We use raw, organic chicken wings and feet with good results. If your animal is older and has compromised teeth, the larger beef soup bones may cause fractures of the teeth. This is another situation where you can dowse to find out which is best for your pet.

Uncooked food always has bacteria on it, even if you wash it, but if your animal is healthy, in most cases, you will see no ill effects. Dowse or muscle test ahead of time to check the effects of raw foods. Go slowly with raw foods of any kind. Let your dog chew his raw bone for 15-20 minutes, then refrigerate it in a baggie until the next day. Throw it out if he isn't finished with it in a couple of days. Too much raw food too fast will lead to diarrhea and vomiting in some cases. So go slowly. With time, you will be able to increase how long he chews his bone and how much raw food he eats.

There are digestive aids available for pets which don't necessarily have vitamins and minerals included, but which aid the digestive process in other ways. If your animal has been ill, has had surgery, been vaccinated or been very stressed, her gut may be imbalanced. The flora may have been killed off, or the pH of the gut may be poor for digestion. We use pre- and probiotics for our animals when we feel they need digestive support. If you have a horse, this type of product is wonderful, as horses are particularly susceptible to colic. Have this or a similar product available at all times and use it regularly if you have a horse or rabbit. Herbivores are a special case, but any animal will benefit from digestive support at times.

Certain conditions will lead to malabsorption, and the nutrients in the food will not be absorbed by your animal, no matter how good they are. Illness, diarrhea, stress, allergies, poisoning and other circumstances can lead to poor absorption. Lack of proper enzymes will contribute to it. Imbalance in intestinal flora also is a factor. Even emotions and noxious environmental energy have an effect on digestion. For example, many horses have ulcers due to stress, lack of exercise and negative emotions.

As you can see, everything is connected in digestion. If you don't have good absorption, it doesn't matter how good the food or supplements are. They won't be processed. So make sure your animal has good basic digestion. If your animal has skin challenges or is having trouble gaining weight, or exhibits other physical symptoms, he may have digestive challenges.

WHICH BRAND AND TYPE?

You want to give your animal friend the best supplement you can. Cheap supplements are less effective, as they are usually made of inorganic minerals that are not easily absorbed by most animals.

In nature, plants remove the inorganic minerals from the soil and chelate (kee-late) them, making them available to the animals that eat them. Feeding your horse dead, colorless straw is not the same as fresh hay, and you can't easily replace the missing minerals by giving your animal calcium carbonate or manganese chloride, which are inorganic (although horses can process a small amount of inorganic minerals, unlike humans).

Many feed companies have jumped on the bandwagon of chelated minerals, because consumers are becoming more educated about nutrition. Unfortunately, not all chelated minerals are equally bioavailable. Chelated minerals are attached to another molecule or substance. If the molecule they are attached to is absorbed easily, they are also taken into the cell.

Proteinates are slightly better than inorganic minerals, but not as good as amino acid chelates or those compounded with fructose, or so current studies say.

Read your labels and make sure you are getting what you paid for. It is worth a bit more to get the best quality. Don't get suckered into just looking at how many milligrams of something are in your supplement. That isn't as important as what form the mineral takes, because the bio-availability determines how much gets into your system.

RDAs are based in many cases on inorganic minerals, and much larger quantities of them are required to stave off malnutrition, because they are not that absorbable. (It's kind of like eating rust to get your iron levels up.) However, any type of chelated minerals are more bioavailable, so that lower amounts of them are better than large amounts of inorganics.

Herbivores in general are able to process inorganic minerals a bit better than carnivores, but should have chelated minerals as well. Also, vitamins have different forms. Vitamin E in particular has been shown to work better when it is the naturally-occurring form, rather than the synthetic type which is cheaper to manufacture.

It is interesting to note that scientific research is beginning to show more applications for minerals than just helping to make enzymes, which are necessary for bodily functions. Minerals are also apparently helpful at removing or lowering levels of toxins in the body. Since toxins seem to predispose the body to or even cause disease, minerals are a vital preventive measure for optimal health.

How to Decide?

In addition to learning about nutritional supplements and reading labels, it is helpful to be able to determine through an intuitive method such as dowsing or muscle testing what supplements your animal needs. A good basic dowsing course will address how to ask appropriate questions on this subject.

Not all bodies are created with equal needs, and no one program fits all animals. Become proactive in your animal's health by learning to determine its individual needs through dowsing or muscle testing.

A Questionnaire about Diet

This is an exercise to give you the opportunity to evaluate how healthy your animal friend's diet is. Answer the following questions.

1. Are you giving your animal unfiltered tap water to drink?

2. Do you buy your animal feeds at the grocery store, pet store or vet's office?

3. Check the label of the food. Does the food have any artificial ingredients, such as preservatives or colors or flavor enhancers?

4. Are there added supplements such as vitamins and minerals?

5. Does the formula have any chelated minerals? (as opposed to inorganic minerals like -oxides or -carbonates)

6. Is sugar or another artificial sweetener in the food? (Corn syrup, molasses and other sweeteners included)

7. Are there any descriptions of the ingredients, such as 'organic', 'human grade', 'pesticide-free' that indicate an attempt has been made to make the food more healthy?

8. Is price your main concern when you buy food for your animals?

9. Have you done any reading or research on the different types of feeding programs for your animal, such as at the library or bookstore or on the internet?

10. Is your animal the picture of perfect health? (He never gets sick, looks terrific, has great energy level and has no allergies or behavioral problems)

There are no right or wrong answers to these questions. They are to make you think about what you feed your animal friend.

Notice if you are just listening to commercials or following the crowd, as opposed to taking the time to learn and make your own decision.

We are so rushed in our culture, we often make excuses and fail to educate ourselves. Once you become educated, don't become inflexible. Be open to new information (as opposed to fads) as it is presented.

Always go back to asking what Mother Nature intended if you are unsure about whether something is good for your animal.

To Vaccinate or Not?

Vaccinations are a part of traditionally accepted regular veterinary care for companion animals. Some vaccinations are required by law. Others are given as a matter of course, regardless of the environment your pet lives in.

Vaccinations are a requirement in most cases to board your animal at a kennel. They may be necessary if you wish to show your animal in competition or participate in a group training class.

We grew up with vaccinations and accepted them as healthy for our animal companions, yet evidence is accumulating concerning side effects of vaccinations that make the thoughtful animal caretaker re-evaluate his feelings about these powerful medical tools. Even the AVMA, the official body for veterinarians, is now recommending reduced schedules for vaccinations.

Why is the opinion changing concerning vaccinations? Perhaps as we have had more time to observe the effects of vaccinations over generations of animals, it is becoming clear that in some cases at least, vaccinations are harmful. Drug companies have always known a few facts that aren't always shared with animal owners.

Vaccinations are not a guarantee that your animal will not catch the disease in question. They hedge your bet so to speak, but are not a 100% proof against illness. This may surprise some pet owners.

Secondly, vaccinations are a powerful drug. Like any drug, they have side effects, and they are known to be more potentially harmful for elderly and physically challenged animals than for young, healthy ones. Yet what do vets do to your new undernourished cat or dog? Vaccinate it right away.

Many vaccinations are given in the same amounts to an animal regardless of size, so a tiny Chihuahua receives the same vaccine as a Great Dane. Dosage is also a factor in side effects. Clearly, this puts smaller animals at risk.

We have observed many detrimental reactions to vaccinations, and we believe that it is time to seriously reconsider the whole concept of vaccination.

Vaccinations can have questionable additives that can lead to problems.

Mercury is an example. Heavy metals like mercury accumulate in the body and lead to nasty symptoms.

Dr. Martin Goldstein's book *The Nature of Animal Healing* has an excellent chapter on vaccinations. The medical establishment is beginning to make some changes in vaccination protocols as the evidence becomes incontrovertible that change is needed.

SUMMARY

1. Don't just follow the crowd concerning vaccinations. Educate yourself about this subject. Ask your veterinarian questions. Get on the internet and find out about particular vaccines. Google "vaccinosis" and read.

2. Study about other ways of protecting your animal from disease, the most valuable of which is to help him develop a healthy immune system.

3. Try to avoid getting too many vaccinations at one time. Don't vaccinate a weak, sick or starving animal if at all possible.

4. If you must vaccinate, don't do it just before boarding your animal or taking him on a trip. Give your animal time to recuperate from the vaccination before you leave.

5. If you vaccinate your animal, support him throughout the process. Help aid his digestion, especially if he is a horse. Do energy work to help mitigate side effects, such as using energy clearing or healing techniques. The homeopathic Thuja is traditionally used to stave off vaccinosis. Consult a professional for details.

6. If your animal has ANY reaction to a vaccination, report it immediately to your vet and make sure the drug company hears about it. The main reason things are so slow to change is that the drug companies have a system in place that takes advantage of the natural human tendency to inertia and laziness. Most drug companies won't talk to you about their product, even though you paid for it. They will insist your vet call them, knowing you won't want to inconvenience your vet, or that they can pressure the vet into not doing anything. When our cat was vaccinated and then titer tested to prove it had immunity to rabies, he failed the test. The test was quite costly, and we felt that we should be reimbursed for that cost as well as the cost of the original vaccination and exam, since their product failed to give our cat immunity. I was told they would only speak to the vet, and our vet was not inclined to call them and complain, so we were out nearly $200. The drug companies claim there is 'no proof', when in reality, they refuse to accept controversial data if at all possible.

7. Don't allow the media to stampede you into vaccinating out of fear. Use your intuition about whether it is right for your animal. If you dowse, this will help you make your decision.

Vaccination is a challenging topic, and there are many strong opinions on it. Educate yourself and then make your decision. Keep an open mind as more information becomes available. Above all, be open to new ways of thinking about health and illness and prevention of disease.

By changing your viewpoint, you will change how you feel about what you once took for granted. Give your intuition an equal place in the decision-making process with your rational mind.

Health Care: Allopathic, Holistic or Both?

There are two major viewpoints on health care and healing. Traditional veterinary care is more aligned with what is termed 'allopathic' medicine. Then there are other styles of health care which tend to be more 'natural' methods, and these are called 'alternative' or 'holistic'.

The 'alternative' methods frequently originate from healing techniques that are far older than veterinary medicine, but many of them come from other cultures and originate from a non-scientific belief system. Our culture, which virtually worships science and regards simple, natural methods as 'backward', often looks askance at 'alternative' healing methods.

One should not overlook the financial issues involved in health care as a motivation for this prejudice. Our current system of health care is far from perfect, and as alternative methods lure clients away from traditional modalities, they are also luring away valuable commerce. In many states, veterinarians, like M.D.s, have managed to legislate a monopoly on health care, because it reduces the competition for health care dollars.

So in a nominally free country, you are not legally allowed in some states to have a non-veterinarian work on your animal's health. This kind of tyranny is allowed to exist simply because people accept it.

In other countries, all methods of healing coexist and people choose whatever type they prefer. It is an interesting paradox that the allopathic medical establishment is promoting legislation in many states to prevent 'ordinary' people from learning alternative techniques such as acupuncture, so that they can have a monopoly on these now-accepted modalities which their profession once regarded as useless.

. . .

EDUCATE **Yourself**

While we value the services that allopathic veterinarians offer, we don't believe that they have all the tools necessary to help restore an animal to perfect health in all cases. Furthermore, we believe the paradigm they operate from relies too much on intervention after health is lost.

We believe that prevention is an important ingredient to wellness, and that you as an animal owner can contribute a lot to your pet's health by becoming more attentive to preventive techniques. You will have to use your best judgment as to what type of health care your animal gets.

We urge you to educate yourself through reading and study and talking to a lot of different people. When making your decision, combine your analytical skills with your gut instinct. Don't be afraid to say that something 'just doesn't feel right'. That can be a valid reason for a particular decision, especially if it is part of a process that also involves using the rational mind. If you dowse, you can confirm your instincts by using this intuitive technique.

We are not advocating that you shun your veterinarian. What we are suggesting is that you become more involved in your animal's health on a daily basis. Learn to dowse or sharpen your intuition some other way. You know your animal better than anyone else. Your animal relies on you to speak for her. That means you need to pay attention to her normal behavior so you can catch symptoms before they become full-blown. Then share your concerns with your health care provider. Ask questions about medicines, treatments and side effects. Participate in decisions that affect your animal's health.

On the rare occasions my bunny Mocha had indigestion, it was easily cured with peppermint or chamomile 'tea' fed to her in her water bottle. She never needed a vet's care, and lived to be almost nine years old.

When I got my dog Roger, I wasn't involved in holistic health care. I knew something was wrong with his back because of the way he walked. I took him to our vet, who X-rayed him and pronounced him fine. I was perplexed, but accepted the diagnosis. After all, he was the expert and I had gotten a positive answer. Why should I complain because the news was good? A few years later, after I became involved in natural healing techniques, I had an animal chiropractor examine and treat Roger. She found that Roger had several misalignments that were longstanding, and it even hurt him to have them adjusted. He required multiple sessions to heal the situation, but it was well worth the effort.

We currently work with a holistic vet to improve the overall health of our pets and to treat naturally whenever possible. But we also have a relationship with an allopathic vet who is open to us using other methods, and when appropriate, we go to her.

Holistic Health Care Methods

The first several methods listed require the care of a professional, and you will probably not be a candidate to learn these techniques yourself. However, towards the second half of the list, there are a number of therapies that are fairly easy to learn. We recommend that you not only go to health care professionals for your animal's care, but learn at least one technique that empowers you to help him stay healthy.

HOMEOPATHY

Homeopathy is an old healing modality that has few negative side effects, and can work wonders. There are some veterinarians who are trained in this practice. We recommend you seek the advice of a professional rather than trying to choose homeopathic remedies yourself, except for simple challenges such as bee stings and simple muscle pain. A homeopathic first aid kit is wonderful to have on hand for emergencies.

HERBS

Animals are very responsive to herbs. They seem to be closer to the plant world than humans, and especially herbivores like rabbits and horses can get great results from the healing power of herbs. In nature, animals will seek out the herb they need to help them get well. Since our pets can't do that for themselves, we can often be of assistance. Some herbs are safe and simple to use, but others are not. Check with a professional herbalist or do a lot of serious studying if you desire to use herbs on your animal.

CHIROPRACTIC

Chiropractic is another physical method that has an effect on the energy body. Animals get their spines out of alignment, and that can lead to physical symptoms and pain. We have had excellent experiences taking our animals (rabbits, cats, dogs and horses) to a veterinary chiropractor.

MASSAGE

Massage is a type of body work that is very helpful for health maintenance. We tend to look on massage as a luxury, but it is actually a very healthy practice that should be used more often. There are simple massage tools and techniques that can be practiced by animal owners, and there are professionals who offer massage for animals.

TTOUCH

TTouch is especially good for animals. This is a hands-on type of energy work that is very healing and relaxing and not that hard to learn. You can learn more at http://www.lindatellingtonjones.com.

Reiki

Reiki is another hands-on healing method that is easy to learn and practice. It is gentle and effective and works at unblocking energy on all levels. Spiritual Healing is similar to Reiki, and works just as effectively. http://www.iarp.org is a good website for finding out about Reiki.

OTHERS

Color, sound and crystal energy also work well with animals. Flower essences are also quite effective. Dowsing is an invaluable tool for determining which, if any, of these therapies is best for your animal's condition.

PREVENTION

Do preventive maintenance on your animal in addition to providing him with an excellent diet and plenty of exercise. Step out of the ordinary routine of ignoring your animal's health until it is gone. Take a more proactive role in the health of your animal companion by learning one or more of the above techniques and applying them regularly as directed.

Such methods, unlike allopathic medicine, are designed for prevention and are more effective if used regularly. Don't only use them when your animal has a problem. Spend the time and money before your animal gets sick, rather than after. You will be pleased with the change it makes in your pet's life.

7

Rescuing Animals

Rescued Animals

IF YOU HAVE OBTAINED your pet through a rescue organization like an animal shelter or Humane Society, your animal has special needs. The same is true if your animal came from a pet shop, a series of previous owners, or a breeder who was not following a careful nutritional program for his breeding stock because of a desire to make a bigger profit.

What do all these animals have in common? Their history is partially or fully a mystery to you. You only know what the seller tells you, and they don't always know everything or may even hide facts.

Animals who have been abandoned, neglected or abused need special emotional support for a long time in order to become fully integrated into your family or have the best possible relationship. The previous chapter on emotional issues discusses this in greater detail.

Animals with these types of backgrounds also have special nutritional requirements. Most animals who are 'rescued' are malnourished, have physical ailments or trauma. Then to top it off, these emotionally disturbed and frightened creatures are vaccinated and sometimes surgically altered within a very short period of their 'rescue'.

When you go to the pound and adopt that cute puppy or cat, you are taking on a project to rehabilitate an animal that has been through a severely traumatizing experience. It won't be enough to buy some grocery store food and hope your animal thrives.

If it is young, it may appear to come around, but over time, if you don't make up for the lacks it has experienced, it will develop physical and / or emotional challenges that become a problem.

HEALTH CHALLENGES

Frequently rescue animals have a huge parasite load, both internal and external. This is merely a reflection of how poor their immune systems are. Healthy animals don't get parasite overloads as a rule. If your animal has worms or ticks, especially if it has been undernourished or has had surgery recently, we don't recommend chemically worming it or using pesticides on it. There are natural ways to deal with parasite issues that won't further depress your animal's immune system or challenge its liver.

Tea tree oil on a Q-tip will cause ticks to drop off your dog. There are various herbal flea powders that repel fleas. The best way to reduce the parasite overload is to make your animal healthy so the parasites aren't happy living there. Use the best food and supplements you can afford. Do various types of energy therapies to unblock energy and raise vitality. These are discussed in a later section.

There are some situations where stronger measures, such as chemical wormers, are required, and this is where using an intuitive method such as dowsing can be very helpful. You don't want to stress your animal's system unnecessarily. Follow your gut instinct rather than just doing whatever everyone else does.

At the time of this writing, it is particularly unfortunate that many chemical wormers used for horses can have very negative side effects. Do not assume that something is safe just because you don't need a prescription for it. Use the gentlest chemical you can for the best effect.

Rescue animals may go through a detoxifying period when they begin to eat and drink well. As their health improves, they may shed out their coats or have other major changes that are a sign of health returning to them. Perhaps gunk will come out of their noses and eyes. They may appear to have a cold. You may even see sores in their mouths, or itching of the skin.

It is important to be aware that when you change an animal to a healthier diet, the body may go through a 'healing crisis', which can mimic a cold or flu. A serious healing crisis can be a bit frightening and send you to the vet, where you get antibiotics that merely load more stuff into the body that will need to be detoxed later. So it is important to be able to tell whether what you are seeing is an illness or a detox reaction.

A detox reaction should be supported, not medicated. An illness requires some type of remedy to restore health. Dr. Martin Goldstein's book *The Nature of Animal Healing* has an excellent chapter on this subject. See the Books relating to Intuitive, Natural Animal Health Care section for more on this book.

Less is More

The key when working with rescue animals is that less is more. You may know the best program to have a dog, cat or horse on. Start slowly.

Support digestion with a probiotic and if possible do a general detoxing once the animal has stabilized (reached appropriate weight and appears healthy). Begin introducing high quality food slowly to an animal if you have a choice.

You can take two weeks or three months to get your animal onto the program you like. Once again, following your intuition is the best guide. Start with the basics and only add other things as needed.

Over time, your animal's coat will shed out, become thicker and probably change color. You might see red highlights it didn't have before, or the blacks will be rich and dark.

The coat is a good indicator of overall health. This process will take at least several months, possibly more.

Sometimes an animal that was undernourished or starving will become overweight when in a good home. This is often a reflection of emotional energies that can be cleared. Then the animal can have a healthier weight. Don't put your pet on a diet to lose weight. First, find out why he or she is fat. It can reflect a physical problem, an emotional problem or a behavior issue. Especially if the animal is overeating due to fear of lack in the future, taking away its food only proves it was correct in feeling deprived. That will not solve the underlying problem.

If you are not a dowser, seek professional dowsing help in resolving these issues and creating a good program for your animal companion.

Our rescue animals continued to improve over the course of the first year or two we had them, and sometimes for longer. It is a source of great satisfaction to help an animal become whole and healthy, and you will find it well worth the effort. Good nutrition and a program of excellent supplements are absolutely essential for helping these animals reach optimal health.

8

Environmental Energies & Their Effect

Geopathic Stress: Noxious Environmental Energies

WE HAVE SPOKEN about energy as an invisible component of our environment that can affect us in many ways. Certain types of energy are known to be harmful, especially in high doses, such as X-rays. Even the sun's radiation is harmful if taken in too large a dose.

There are many types of energy that have not been studied fully by modern science, yet have been acknowledged for many years in other cultures as having a detrimental effect.

These particular energies emanate from the earth or are natural in origin. They lead to what is called 'geopathic stress'. Geopathic stress in itself doesn't harm people, but it depresses the immune system, leading to many unpleasant symptoms. Studies, mainly in Europe, have linked geopathic stress to cancer and other diseases. In some European countries, a place must be certified free of geopathic stress before building can commence on it.

Geopathic stress can be present anywhere. It can affect any living thing. The tricky part is that it doesn't affect all living things in the same fashion.

In fact, for example, certain energies are bad for humans, but good for cats. This is merely a reflection of the fact that energy itself is neutral, and that we are placing a judgment on it based on how it affects us. It is even true that a given noxious environmental energy won't affect all humans the same way. Each person is an individual and may respond differently to any given energy based on their genetic makeup, health and stress level, among other things. This is one reason that environmental effects have been hard to quantify.

Years ago, a client called to tell us most of her 12 horses were exhibiting signs of colic. These horses were on an excellent nutritional program and they were not responding to her efforts. We quickly dowsed that a space clearing was needed, as some geopathic stress had developed that had energetically contaminated her hay. After the clearing was completed, all of the horses recovered from their symptoms.

The night before, one of her horses had died of colic. A chemical evaluation revealed no contaminants on the hay, further validating our assessment that it was energetic in nature.

Be Sensitive to the Possibility

Dowsing is a great way to detect noxious environmental energies. There are many ways of clearing such detrimental energies from the environment. Among the most common are sound, fragrance, symbols and intention.

If you or your animal has developed symptoms only since moving to a new location, it is possible that geopathic stress/noxious environmental energy is the cause. Dowsing or muscle testing will be helpful in evaluating this. If your animal friend has a symptom or behavior that has not responded to a change in diet, water, medication or routine, perhaps she is suffering from geopathic stress.

It is hard for animals to describe their symptoms to humans. We must become more sensitive and aware for them. We have seen many radical changes result from clearing noxious environmental energies.

ENVIRONMENTAL ENERGY: **Man-Made**

Besides natural energies that can be detrimental to the health and well-being of your animal companion, there are manmade energies that are potentially harmful. Most of these energies are electromagnetic frequencies, and thus are called EMF. Any power source can put out detrimental energy. Clock radios and microwave ovens are familiar sources of such energies. Transformers, power lines and microwave towers are some that may be found outdoors in your neighborhood.

As mentioned earlier, not all species respond the same to a given energy. Some will find a particular energy noxious, while others may be attracted to it and find it beneficial. Dowsing and muscle testing are helpful tools in sorting out the effects of various energies on the animals in your family.

DETECTION AND CURE

Dowsing may be used to identify sources that are harmful to you and your pets. There are then many possible ways of transforming the energy or protecting you and your animals from it. Devices that protect against various types of noxious energy may be purchased on the internet.

Space clearing is widely gaining recognition as important in health issues. There are many professional space clearers. If you learn to dowse and study about space clearing, you can maintain your own space to a great extent.

We recommend checking with a professional periodically to make sure you haven't missed anything if you do your own clearings.

Human and Other Energies

While the environment can have detrimental energies that come from the earth or man-made equipment, there is another large potential source of detrimental energy for your animal (and you). When you interact and live with other humans or animals, you are subject to each other's energy fields.

Your animal friend probably has close contact with you physically. Your dog may sleep on your bed. Your cat may like to nap in your favorite chair. You ride your horse. These and other similar situations can allow the transfer of negative energies from you to your animal.

Just like a bad cold or the flu, energies are transferred invisibly. When two living things are physically close, there is the opportunity to exchange energies.

The same is true if you have multiple animals in your family. They can exchange energies with each other. Even when you think about someone, you can create an energetic connection that allows the transfer of negative energies in some cases.

Negative energies, for example, fear, can create behavior problems if the charge on them gets large enough. The best way to improve such situations is to clear the negative energies. This has been discussed in an earlier section. There are a number of techniques you can use to clear these energies, or have professionals work with you.

THE ANIMAL-HUMAN DYNAMIC

Animals can also act as mirrors of our own energetic circumstances.

Dr. Martin Goldstein comments on animals having similar physical symptoms to their owners in his book, *The Nature of Animal Healing*. We have also found that an animal will sometimes behave a certain way or have a certain symptom as a message to its human.

We worked with a dog who had ear problems that turned out to be related to his owner's need to 'listen' to her Inner Self. She recognized the message after we brought it to her attention. She dealt with it, and her dog's ears got well. While this isn't always the case, it is common with animals who have a long and close relationship with their humans.

You may recall the two examples in the Behavior section about my animals who had dental issues. Dental issues often reflect a need to make a decision, and these problems came at a critical time in my life when I needed to make some major changes.

The energetic dynamics of the human-animal relationship are very complex and not fully recognized by our culture. If you accept that you are connected with your pet, you will be able to look at his or her issues and perhaps discover whether they are a message to you, or a plea for a clearing of some type.

Situations that do not respond well to traditional treatments aimed at the physical body often respond well to modalities that address underlying energies. Another situation we have often seen with pets is that they sometimes choose to take on and process negative energies to protect their human. In some cases, such as serious environmental noxious energy, the result was fatal.

In most cases, such altruism results in long term illness or degenerative symptoms that can be very painful and don't respond to treatment. Once you accept that this is possible and you become aware, you can then follow your intuition or dowse to find what the appropriate course of action is.

The bottom line is that there are usually energetic causes at the root of all problems, both with us and with our animals.

Clearing Energy

We have discussed the concept of blocked energy in a previous section. All living things require a flow of life force energies to enjoy health and wholeness. When energy is lacking or stagnant or blocked, health can be poor, emotions can be erratic and life can be very difficult.

This is true both for you and your animal companions of any species. Physical symptoms often are outward manifestations of blocked or low energy.

While going to a health care professional may give relief for the symptom, you probably won't heal the condition completely until you determine the ultimate cause energetically. That can be very challenging, so most people settle for taking an 'aspirin' to relieve the pain.

Auras and Chakras

You have many energy centers in your body, as does your animal, called 'chakras'. These chakras are energetic transformers that help convert the life force energy into physically usable form. Just as your body requires physical sustenance to survive, you also need adequate energy to live.

If your chakras are not functioning well or if you have energetic blockages or leaks, you will have physical symptoms. There are many techniques for identifying energetic problems and resolving them.

You may have seen a picture of an aura in a book, or if you are lucky, you may have had your own aura photographed. The aura is believed to offer a protective layer around your physical body. Damage to the aura can lead to physical problems. The aura changes constantly as your chakras and energy level change. These changes may appear photographically as certain colors. All living things have auras, and many people are capable of seeing them.

There are books available that teach you how to 'see' auras if you are interested in learning this intuitive technique.

ENERGETIC TECHNIQUES

Other methods are less visual, but can gather lots of information about the energy body. Various types of hands-on healing techniques, such as Reiki and Spiritual Healing, use the hands to sense the energetic condition of a person or animal, and to channel life force energy into the body for balancing and healing.

These techniques access what is sometimes termed the 'universal life force energy' to stimulate the body's self-healing response. Those who practice these techniques intuitively sense energy blockages, aura damage and other energetic conditions that are harmful to the physical body.

In an earlier section the concept of detrimental environmental energies were covered in some detail. 'Space clearing' can be accomplished using intuitive techniques such as dowsing to identify noxious energy sources and then determine the best method to clear them. By clearing and transforming such energies, many positive changes can occur in both humans and animals.

Personal energies resulting from past lives or the current lifetime can have a negative effect on you and / or your pet. We have had countless experiences with health and behavior problems of clients that were alleviated or completely resolved through the use of appropriate personal clearing methods.

By clearing negative energies from your system, you remove the 'magnets' that attract unwanted events into your life. The same is true for your animal friend. An awareness of and respect for 'energy' can enhance our relationship with our animal companions. Both yours and your animal's physical and emotional health are affected by the energies in your environment and the energies within you.

These energies can best be detected, balanced and cleared using intuitive methods. By becoming more intuitive yourself, you will be able to take responsibility for this important aspect of your life with your animal friend.

9

Karma & Reincarnation

Keep An Open Mind

THE WORD 'KARMA' is familiar enough in our culture, yet it is not clearly understood or taken seriously by most people. Karma refers to the natural consequences of actions. Everything you do has a consequence. Sometimes what may appear to be an inconsequential event turns out to have tremendous impact on your life.

Reincarnation is a belief of the majority of the world's population, though it is a minority belief in Western culture and religion. Reincarnation refers to the belief that a given soul lives in material form multiple times rather than just one lifetime as is the current Christian belief.

How do these 'New Age-y' concepts relate to your relationship with your animal companion, and how is intuition involved in them?

We believe that events in past lives can affect the course of a current life, for humans and animals. We have frequently seen unexplained health and emotional issues clear once past life energies or beliefs were cleared.

Perhaps the negative energies that we have discussed previously are the manifestation of karma in this life time. The negative energies we hold on an event, past or present, attracts more of the same to us. Maybe by clearing these energies, we clear karma.

We had a horse client who had been ailing for nearly two years. Her owners were caring, committed individuals who used excellent methods of nutrition and hoof care in an effort to restore the mare's health. Her feet were a constant source of pain, and she would rally a bit, then backslide to a poor level of health. Many would have put her down because she seemed unable to heal. When they came to us, the couple had tried everything they could think of to help the horse.

In my original communication session with her, the mare showed me a past life when she had been a unicorn, and humans had mutilated her to take her horn. Strangely enough, her problems had become serious in this life when the vet had scored both hooves in a technique he thought would relieve pressure, but instead sent her into a downward spiral.

I was uneasy about revealing this information to these new clients whom I did not know well, but I told them anyway. The owner pulled a chain from under her sweater, and on it was a unicorn. She then handed me her business card, which had a unicorn logo. I had not been aware of her interest in unicorns.

She confessed that she had felt that the mare and she were specially bonded, and my feeling was that they had been together in a past life. When Nigel spoke with the mare, she said she didn't feel she could get well. She had been sick so long, she couldn't picture being well. We were able to dowse to find some methods that brought some significant improvement in her condition.

· · ·

Intuition

Intuition is an important part of understanding these concepts and how they affect your relationship with your pet. You can't sense these things using your five physical senses, but there are many methods of intuitively accessing information related to past lives and the energies associated with them that are affecting you now.

Dowsing, tarot cards and the I Ching are just a few of the methods by which you can find out more about these subjects. Some of the earlier clearing methods we have used, such as Senzar clearing and Spiritual Response Therapy, also access information from past lives that can be affecting humans and animals in their current lives. All of these methods tap into your intuitive senses (or those of the practitioner).

You may intuitively know that you have an unusual connection with one of your animal friends. It may surpass the normal attraction and love you have for your other pets. It is almost as if you have known each other before, and that when you first met, you knew you belonged together, or at least you knew you had a special connection.

This was the case with my dog, Roger, who has been with me in at least one previous life. I have a very close connection with him. He follows me like a shadow. His biggest fear in this lifetime is that of abandonment, and indeed I had to go abroad for ten months and leave him in someone's care, even though I didn't want to have to leave him.

Had I been aware of the clearing methods we now use, I could have prevented a lot of heartache, which I believe is a repeat of what he experienced in past lives with me.

ANIMALS AS MESSENGERS

Sometimes an animal comes back into your life multiple times to support you and help you. Animals can be earth angels, and there are plenty of books written to confirm that. Other times, they may appear again and again to help you to learn to make a change in your life that will bring you closer to happiness. It may be a simple change is required, such as for the people who kept replacing dogs who were hit by cars. Their dogs were giving them messages about boundaries, but they were unheeded.

Sometimes, as we have discussed, animals can mirror our own issues and emotions (karma) so that we can have the opportunity to deal with them. Whether that emotion is fear, anger or loneliness, we may be too judgmental towards ourselves or not tuned in enough to realize we need help. By reflecting these energies, our animal companions let us know we need to work on these things so that we can be happier.

Our animal companions are an integral part of the complex web of our lives, both physically and energetically. They are helpers, teachers, guides and mirrors. These purposes often connect them to us over the course of many lifetimes, and you can use your intuition, or intuitive methods, to learn more about the role of your animal friend in your current and past lives.

10

Help from Fairies and Angels

Invisible Helpers

MOST PEOPLE HAVE HEARD of angels and fairies, which are common forms of spiritual beings that are very helpful to humans and animals. The realm of fairies and nature spirits is complex and varied. Those who work with the earth in any form, whether as miners, fishers or farmers, can benefit from a better understanding of these beings.

Angels and devas may be regarded as different 'levels' of spiritual beings from fairies. They are commonly thought of as 'higher' beings, as their functions seem to be at levels 'above' fairies and other nature spirits. There are many types of nature spirits with many different functions.

When working with animals, fairies and angels seem to be of particular assistance. You can get their help just by asking. I ask for the help of both angels and fairies when I communicate with an animal or when I am trying to help an animal in any way. They can be good intermediaries when dealing with a wild animal or an animal that doesn't know you well. If you are using an intuitive technique of any type, they can help you achieve a greater level of success than you would on your own.

There are oracle cards for getting information from angels and fairies, and they can often be applied to situations that include your animal companion. I have made my own set of cards specifically for issues relating to companion animals that I think is more comprehensive. Oracle cards are a great intuitive method for accessing information about your relationship with your animal friend.

When you consciously begin to use your intuition in your relationship with your pet, you will find that it is easier to accept the possibility that such things as angels and fairies exist. When you see the wonderful results you can get by working with them, you will be glad you set your rational mind aside long enough to experience such excellent assistance. This is perhaps the ultimate test of becoming more intuitive in the care of your animal friend: asking you to work with unseen helpers.

11

Dowsing: A Valuable Intuitive Technique

What Is Dowsing?

DOWSING, what we call Natural Knowing, is an intuitive method of getting information from your environment. You may use a tool when dowsing, such as a pendulum, or you may just sense your answer through your body, as in 'deviceless dowsing'.

We use dowsing daily for many purposes, and it is highly beneficial when working with animals, as they are unable to tell us in their own words what they are feeling. If you use kinesiology or muscle testing, you are doing the same thing as dowsing. Muscle testing uses a muscular response to give information.

Dowsing may be done in person or long distance. This may be a challenging concept, but you use many things daily that you don't understand. For example, people know that radio and television work over long distances, yet they don't understand how.

Although the way dowsing works is not understood, it can give very accurate responses over great distances. An example is many water dowsers dowse over maps, at least initially, to locate ideal places to drill wells.

LEARNING to Use Your Natural Knowing Power

Everyone has the ability to tap into their Natural Knowing Power. Let's give you a few examples of how you can get started getting answers to questions. We will describe two of our favorite techniques. There are many to choose from, and you can visit our websites for more details and free lessons.

THE BODY SWAY

Stand with your body straight, feet shoulder width apart. Close your eyes to accentuate the perception of movement. Relax. Empty your mind of judgment or emotion. Now think or say out loud, "I was born in _____in this lifetime." Fill in the blank with the place of your birth.

Note what your body does. If it appeared to do nothing, relax and try again, focusing on the question with curiosity.

For most people, the body will sway forward to some degree. Forward usually indicates true, healthy and yes.

Now say or think the same statement and substitute a wrong place of your birth. Note how differently your body moves. For most people, it will sway back to some extent. Backwards usually indicates false, unhealthy or no as an answer.

It is beyond the scope of this book to go into a lot of detail, but if you did not get the usual response, or you got no response at all, there will be a reason, and it can be resolved. For the time being, just try the next method and see how it works for you.

$$\cdot \quad \cdot \quad \cdot$$

THE BLINK

Sit in a relaxed position, staring with soft focus at some distant point. It is better that it be something like a blank wall, rather than something of interest. When you feel you are totally relaxed, blink your eyes a few times, release any emotion and ask the question about your birthplace from the previous example, inserting your place of birth in the blank. Note what your eyelids do.

For most people, the eyes try to blink once for yes/true.

Now substitute a false place of birth and repeat the exercise. Note how differently your eyes behave. Most people get no blink response for no/false.

Your responses for both methods may differ from the usual. The important thing is that you get two different responses for 'yes' and 'no'. You need to be able to tell what is 'yes' and what is 'no' in a consistent fashion. Experiment to determine your 'yes' and 'no' responses, then go on to other questions.

Start with small questions which interest you, but do not inspire fear or worry. Build your confidence through practice. Join us on our websites and become confident and reliable in accessing your Natural Knowing/Dowsing answers.

Dowsing tools may be purchased through organizations or through our website. There are also many books available on how to dowse and the uses of dowsing, including our own. We also have a free online dowsing community. See the Resources section for details.

Learning to dowse will put you in touch with your intuitive faculties, as it is an intuitive method. By becoming confident and accurate at accessing information through your intuition, you will have a more balanced approach in your relationship with your animals and to life in general.

It is true that becoming a dowser can change your life in ways you can't begin to imagine. It did for us. The next section will give you specific uses of dowsing to help animals.

Dowsing/Natural Knowing to Help Animals

There are countless ways to use dowsing to help animals. The major ones are listed here.

1. Detecting and clearing noxious environmental energies: You can locate detrimental energies in your living space and that of your pet using dowsing. Then you can dowse to find the best method to clear the energies or transform them.

2. Dietary programs: All animals, like humans, are individuals, with their own preferences and sometimes with sensitivities or allergies to certain foods. You can use dowsing to evaluate the water and food you are feeding your animal, and to select a better grade of food that will be more healthy and palatable to your pet.

3. Supplements: There are many dietary supplements for pets these days. Use dowsing to evaluate the vitamins, minerals and other supplements you are buying or considering buying for your animal friend. All things change over time. You can use dowsing to determine if the brand you have been using for two months is indeed what your animal now needs.

4. Medicines, prescription and nonprescription: Dowsing is an excellent way of determining the level of side effects and the efficacy of medications. Allergies and negative side effects to drugs are fairly commonplace. If you can dowse, you can determine whether a medication is going to cause a negative reaction in your animal companion, how intense the reaction will be and if he or she can tolerate it.

5. Therapies of all kinds: There are a plethora of therapies available for animals these days, both allopathic and holistic. Since all animals are individuals, they don't all respond equally well to any given therapy. If you can dowse, you can predict which therapy will be most effective

for your pet and will have the least negative side effects. You can use dowsing to see if there will be a detox reaction or an allergic response.

6. Therapists of all kinds: Use dowsing to select a veterinarian or therapist for your pet.

7. Surgical and other procedures, including vaccinations: Some of these things are optional, and some are not. Dowsing will prepare you for whatever the consequences of the procedure are. If you discover your animal will not fare well with a vaccination or surgery, you may be able to elect to postpone it or find an alternative. If that is not an option, you can use dowsing to determine the intensity of the reaction, and what you can do to help your animal recover.

8. Breeding programs: Not all animals should be bred. Either they don't want to, or they are not going to produce the offspring you would like. Dowsing will help you determine if an animal should be part of your breeding program. Then you can plan your program using dowsing to select the appropriate mating combinations.

9. Shows and competition: Not all animals should compete. They either don't want to, or they are not fit to for some reason. Dowse to find out if your animal wants to participate in competition. Then you can determine the best type of competition for your animal through dowsing. You can also dowse to see which shows you should participate in.

10. Training programs: Use dowsing to see how the animal feels about participating in the training program. Evaluate trainers and programs through dowsing.

11. Behavioral issues: Dowsing can be used to determine the cause of behavioral problems. It can also help you find a solution.

12. Physical challenges: Energetic causes of physical symptoms may be revealed through dowsing.

13. Finding lost animals: When an animal gets lost, you can use dowsing to find her, if she wants to be found.

14. Communication: Dowsing may be used to communicate directly with an animal. You simply connect with the animal you want to talk with, once you have his permission, and ask questions in a `yes' or `no' format.

15. You can dowse to communicate with the angels and fairies to get their help with your animals.

You may be able to think of other ways of using dowsing to help your animal friends. The more you do this, the more intuitive you will become in relating to your animal. A more intuitive relationship is a more natural one, and you will be empowering yourself immensely by using this tool.

Learn the Best Way to Solve Pet Problems

Maybe you can relate to this: we have been lifelong animal lovers who have rescued and nurtured many animal companions over the years. But like other pet owners, we had problems with our animals: destructive chewing, health issues, excessive barking, inappropriate urination.

We read books, talked to experts and tried all kinds of things. And what we learned over the years was that the best thing we could do to get problems solved was to approach them in a new way.

That new way involved connecting to the intuitive side of our brains, our Natural Knowing. We used a Natural Knowing technique called Dowsing.

Because this has worked wonders for us, we want to share our expertise about Natural Knowing/Dowsing with you that will help you tap into the innate ability you have to find solutions to the problems in your life, even those that don't include your animal friends.

This technique has literally saved lives, money and heartache for us, and we know it can do the same for you.

PLEASE LEAVE A REVIEW

We would appreciate it if you would take the time to review our book wherever you made your purchase.

APPENDICES

ALL THE QUESTIONNAIRES AND COMMUNICATION EXERCISE

Intuition Self-Test

This test is very simple, but it is important that you take it with the appropriate frame of mind, or your results will be meaningless.

Please select answers that represent your own personal preference. Do *NOT* select answers that you feel are right based on anything external to you, such as what you do to succeed at work, what is expected of you from friends and family, or what society thinks you should value.

These external values are often different from personal preferences, and you will not get an accurate score if you select answers based on what you think you SHOULD like or prefer, or what you HAVE to do to survive in society.

For more information on personality testing, see the Resources section for titles and links.

Answer 'yes' or 'no' to the following questions :

1. *Do you prefer getting an idea of the 'big picture' rather than having to get bogged down in tiny details?* (For example, do you tend to skip reading instructions unless you absolutely have to?)

2. *Do you frequently skip logical steps in the thinking process, arriving at conclusions with the help of insight and hunches?* (If so, you probably find it tedious to listen to what seem like obvious step-by-step presentations, because you usually see what is being aimed at in advance.)

3. *Do you tend to view relationships optimistically, seeing what is possible rather than what is really there now?*

4. *When at work, do you like to learn new skills and new ways of doing things, rather than always using the 'tried and true' methods that have sufficed in the past?*

5. *Do the words/phrases 'sixth sense, theoretical, future possibilities and insights' attract you more than the words/phrases 'facts, practical, what is real and the five senses'?*

6. *Do you enjoy reading for pleasure and working with computers?*

7. *When traveling in a new place, do you tend to get general impressions about your surroundings, rather than noting details? Do you tend to give directions that relate to landmarks, partly because you find yourself bemused about compass directions when in a strange place (e.g., 'travel 6 blocks north' seems absurd to you)?*

8. *Do you feel that whatever is, can be better or different, and thus you find yourself focusing on possibilities for improving things?*

9. *Do you sometimes or often make decisions based purely on a gut feeling, and later find out you were right?*

Scoring

Each 'yes' answer represents a choice for the use of intuition over the five senses. The higher your score, the greater your preference for the intuitive senses.

This does not mean you exercise your intuition to an extreme, but that it is your preference. You may behave differently in your relationships or at work than is your preference, but this test is meant to demonstrate your natural inclinations, which may also be reflected in your perceived abilities and experiences with respect to intuition.

Indeed, if you have very many or very few 'yes' answers, it would be wise of you to beware of exercising your preference too much, whichever that is. We all have both intuitive and physical sensing capabilities, and it is best to combine the two types of methods of interacting with the environment, rather than relying on one alone.

In this book, you will be asked to exercise your intuition, which we believe will aid you in developing a better relationship with your animal companions. In our culture, intuition has been devalued to the point that many people don't trust their gut feelings. We believe that if you have a viewpoint that incorporates intuition, you will have a more balanced and successful relationship with animals.

Choosing A Pet: Rational Choice

The following questions are designed to make you think about your choice of an animal companion in a logical, reasonable way. It is critical that you answer these questions honestly for best results.

Comments after each question are to help you see why these subjects are important to your relationship with your pet.

1. *Do you spend a lot of time outdoors participating in activities that are very physical?* If you enjoy outdoor activities, you may prefer an animal that can join you in your interests. A horse or dog would possibly be a good choice.

2. *Are you more of an indoors person, who likes to read and watch TV in your spare time?* Anything from a fish, turtle or bird to a cat or possibly a dog might serve your needs.

3. *Are you living in rented space where you have to be extra cautious about damage?* Animals that live in cages, like birds, guinea pigs, rabbits, hamsters, fish and reptiles may be best for you.

4. *Do you live in a high density location, like a city apartment complex, or a rural setting with a great deal of open space?* Animals like dogs, horses and even cats need a fair amount of exercise to be healthy. Consider how much you can provide where you live.

5. *Is your living space very casually appointed, with secondhand furniture, or do you have fine antiques and valuable design artifacts?* Puppies, kittens, dogs and cats can be terribly destructive. If that will bother you, then perhaps a bird, fish, reptile or other caged animal will be a safe bet for you.

6. *Do you spend a lot of time at home during the day? During the evening? On weekends?* The more time you spend, the better. Any type of animal needs your attention. If you aren't home much, then you probably shouldn't have an animal dependent on you, unless it is something very simple like fish or reptiles.

7. *Do you live with other people? If so, what sex and ages are they?* Small children are not always compatible with dogs and cats. Small dogs are not necessarily safer for children than large ones. In fact, in my experience, the opposite is often true. Much supervision is required when small children live with animals. Don't get a pet if you can't commit to that.

8. *Does everyone you live with like animals? Are there any allergies to animals, fear of animals, or other reasons that would make a pet an issue?* You must consider everyone in your living space when you are getting a pet. Check phobias and allergies as well as personal preferences before acquiring your companion animal. If you have a long-standing animal relationship that is in conflict with a current boy or girlfriend, then maybe you need to reconsider the relationship (with the boyfriend/girlfriend).

9. *Will this animal be the only pet you have, or do you have others? If others, what type are they? How do they like other animals of this type? How can you be sure?* Consider the feelings of your other animal companions before you get a new friend. Older dogs and cats often

feel put upon when a new kitten or puppy comes along. Sometimes, however, it gives them a new lease on life. It is wise to consult the pet directly for their preference. If you can't ask them yourself, hire an animal communicator to ask them.

10. *Is your weather sunny, warm and dry, or cold and wet? Is it extreme in any way?* If your animal has to live outdoors (this is not desirable for many) or spend a lot of time outdoors with you, then you need to make sure it is suited to your climate. A Newfoundland is not bred for desert weather, nor is a greyhound likely to enjoy Alaskan winters. Find out about the climate that best suits the breed of animal you are considering. Most likely, this will be the climate they originally were bred to live and work in.

11. *What do you like about the idea of having a pet? Have you lived with this type of animal before (the one you are considering getting)? Does this type of animal lend itself to your dream?* Examine your reasons for getting a pet. Make sure they are grounded in reality and that you are compatible with this type of animal.

12. *How much time do you have each day to devote to training, grooming, feeding, exercising and playing with your animal friend? Do you have time to take it for health care when needed?* Don't get a longhaired cat or dog if you don't want to brush it. Don't get a shedding dog if hair all over the place bothers you. Dogs and cats and horses require training. Don't get one if you don't have the time, interest and money to do so.

13. *Do you like doing things for an animal like brushing, nail trimming, tooth brushing, bathing, hair trimming, etc?* Even if you have the time and money to groom and train your pet, is it something you really want to do? If not, reconsider your choice.

14. *Have you done any research on the health requirements, training needs and behavior of this type of animal? If so, how much?* Educate yourself about the species of animal you are thinking of purchasing. You might be amazed at the amount of care most animals need. It isn't

enough to just feed and walk a dog. Animals require dental care, grooming, training, exercise and love. Horses in particular are very labor-intensive to maintain properly.

15. *Are you a laid-back type of person or a perfectionist? How easily irritated are you by messes, noise, frustration and accidents that involve damage to things you value?* If you are a highly irritable person, then a dog or cat probably isn't for you. They will try your patience too much. Get some help with your challenges before acquiring an animal that might aggravate you.

16. *Are you demonstrative and affectionate or more reserved? Are you embarrassed to talk out loud to your animal friend, even in private?* The more intelligent an animal, the more important it is for you to talk with it and express yourself in some fashion. More reserved people might prefer animals that don't demand interaction as much as dogs and cats do.

17. *Do you feel like animals have emotions somewhat like humans? Do you empathize with them easily? Are you a nurturing person?* You may be an excellent person to help foster homeless animals or raise orphaned ones. Animals that seek interaction may be better suited to you than independent ones.

18. *What are your finances like? Do you have more than enough money to provide good quality food, training, grooming, health care and boarding when required?* If you're not sure, then you aren't ready to take on the responsibility of a dependent animal. It always costs more than you think to take on a dependent if you intend to do things right. Make sure you can commit to doing what an animal needs to have a healthy lifestyle. If money is tight, you can still own a small animal and enjoy the benefits of pet ownership, but you may want to avoid dogs, cats and horses, which are higher maintenance animals.

19. *Are you prepared for a long-term commitment to this animal? Do you know the average life span? Can you see yourself with this animal for that long?* DON'T get an animal thinking you can always give it away or sell it if you change your mind. Do your best to commit to caring for an animal for life, but be aware that things sometimes happen that change your abilities to do so. Don't put a burden on yourself, but don't be thoughtless, either. Going from home to home or owner to owner is very taxing and stressful on an animal. Plan on keeping your animal for her entire life if possible. Don't treat it like a piece of furniture.

20. *Are you easily provoked to physical violence when angry?* If so, it would be best NOT to acquire an animal companion. Instead, seek counseling to learn to express your anger in other ways before bringing an animal into your life.

21. *Are you under a lot of stress in your life at the current time?* If so, it is NOT advisable to get a pet at this time. There are many ways to work on stress management that can reduce your stress levels, but getting a pet is NOT one of them if your stress level is high. There is too great a risk that your animal will either contribute to the stress you feel by its demands on your time and money, or that you will use your animal as an outlet for stress-related emotions that are not healthy for the animal. Furthermore, animals always reflect our current conditions, and a stressed-out pet can be destructive or ill.

Choosing A Pet: Intuitive Factors

You will be asked to think about some subjects that relate to your choice of animal friend from an intuitive view point. This will not be as linear and straightforward as the previous exercise, because it is intuitive.

As with the other evaluation, there are no right or wrong answers. These questions are merely to motivate you to think intuitively about the decision you are getting ready to make.

1. *How do you relate to animals?*

Have they always been a part of your life, so that you feel incomplete without one by your side? Some people are animal people. Still others go beyond that, and are cat persons, or horse persons, based on their favorite species. Think about how you feel about animals. Have you always felt that way? Are they important to you, or can you live happily without them? Does your desire to have a pet stem from a driving **NEED** or simply a wish to have a companion? Your actual answer is not as important as your motivation for it. Think carefully about how you feel about animals. Don't get a pet just because you always have had one, or because you are desperately lonely. Make sure you actively want to have an animal in your life. Pets are not child or significant other-substitutes. They are animal friends.

2. *Why are you choosing this particular type of animal?*

Have you always wanted a black horse or a yellow dog? Is it because your friend has a great animal that you like, and you want to have a similar relationship? Are you being forced to adopt an animal by your children or spouse, but you don't really want one? Is a relative or friend trying to convince you to take on their animal, because they no longer need, want or can care for it? 'Why' is an important question. Sometimes it is hard to be honest. Listen to your heart. What does it tell you about getting an animal companion?

3. *Examine your feelings about this decision.*

Are you getting a pet out of guilt, obligation, pressure or envy? Don't do it. Do you feel calm about doing this? Excited? Afraid? Examine all your feelings about this choice. You will probably have many. A feeling solely of excitement may mean you are doing this for the emotional high it gives you. Make sure you feel grounded, calm and peaceful about the decision as well. Examine any feelings of fear, and make sure they aren't a signal from your intuition that this is the wrong time, place or choice for you. A tight, churning feeling in your gut usually means you shouldn't do it.

4. *Are you rushing to make this purchase?*

If so, you may be subconsciously trying to override your intuitive feelings that this is not a good choice. Slow down, take your time. Listen to your heart and pay attention to the signs your body gives you about what you are considering.

5. Have you always wanted this particular type of animal in your life, or is it a sudden new interest?

Be careful either way. Get in touch with your feelings about this decision. Are you trying to make a childhood dream come true? Why? Don't get a pony just because you are mad your parents never got you one. Maybe they were right. Even if they weren't, they were doing the best they could at the time. If your interest is recent, are you sure it isn't some fad you are jumping on the bandwagon to join?

6. Do you resonate with this particular type of animal?

Does everything about it 'ring true' to you? Can you easily see yourself living with this animal as a companion for many years? Do you have a strong desire to inter act with this animal: ride your horse, play with a dog, stroke a cat? Good. You are on the right track.

Advanced Communication Technique

Communicating with animals in more advanced ways requires an intuitive perspective rather than a rational, scientific one. If you are a logical person who is oriented to things you can perceive with your five physical senses, then this type of communication may be challenging to you. However, you *CAN* learn to do it.

For those who are naturally more intuitive and sense things beyond the physical senses, this may be a bit easier. The bottom line is that anyone can learn to do this if they want to.

Setting the Scene

For beginners, it is important to be relaxed and have a location conducive to accessing this natural ability. Don't attempt this if you are tired, stressed or feeling any strong emotion such as anger, irritation, sadness or fear. Make sure you are fully hydrated. Wear loose-fitting clothing. Sit in a chair that is good support for your back but also comfortable. Find a quiet space.

Experienced communicators can do this anywhere, but as a beginner, you want to give yourself every advantage you can. You are creating an environment that will allow you to hear your Inner Voice, which is usually quiet in most people, stilled by years of ignoring it.

Many people have switched polarity, due to exposure to manmade sources of electromagnetic energy or other factors. You can restore your polarity by taking the first two fingers of your right hand and drawing them across your forehead from right to left three times with the intention of restoring your polarity. This will usually restore your polarity, and it won't harm anything if your polarity is correct to begin with.

You may play soft music during the session if you like. It should not have any lyrics. New Age type music works well, as it won't intrude on what you are doing.

Close your eyes while you are doing the session. By blocking the stimuli coming in visually, you remove some distractions. Set your intention to have your left brain or rational side to sit back and stay out of the session. Assure it that you will be needing and using it again later, but you don't want to create confusion by trying to use analysis during the session.

Your intent should be to stay totally open to whatever comes in, without interpreting it or analyzing it in any way. Further set your intention *NOT* to be influenced or affected by any personal prejudices you may have. Complete openness will enhance your results. You can analyze them after the session.

Focus on your breathing with your eyes closed. Breathe in and out, filling your lungs deeply. When you feel totally relaxed, you may begin the exercise, or you may have a friend read the written version provided on the next page.

Don't Try to Rush Anything!

The first time you do this exercise, let it be solely for the purpose of creating your safe place and 'furnishing' it as you like. Meet your helpers or guides that first time and bond with them. The next time you go through the exercise, you can then feel prepared to speak with an animal. (This technique can also be used to get information from plants and nonliving objects of any kind.)

You may alter the chakra balancing part of the exercise as you wish with subsequent sessions. The 'rainbow' part of the exercise helps you to balance yourself energetically and activate your intuitive senses. As you become more adept at this type of communication, feel free to alter the method to suit your needs.

In addition to preparing your location to enhance your experience, there are some other points that are important to remember. You are asking permission to communicate with your subjects, whoever or whatever they are. If they decline, thank them and send them back. If they leave in the middle of a session, thank them and bring out another subject. If a subject is reserved, respect that and treat him or her as you would a very shy human.

Preparing your questions in advance can be helpful, but don't feel you have to stick to a script. Always thank your subjects when you are through, and thank your helpers.

After the Session

When the session is over, very quickly write your results down, because you may find you forget details as you return to a more physically conscious state. If you have someone guiding you through the session, they can write the answers as you get them.

When you analyze your results after a session, do not spend much time wondering if you made up the answers yourself. Accept them and try to find a way to make sense of them.

Do not become discouraged if your results are less than perfect at first. This takes practice. Also, some subjects are better and more cooperative than others. Start with an animal that is an extrovert who loves you a lot, and you may find you get more detailed answers to your questions. Then progress to shy animals or strangers. They frequently talk less in the initial session due to a natural reserve.

Although this technique has basic elements that should always be present for best results, much of the form of it can be changed to suit your preferences. Follow your intuition to alter whatever you wish, and you can improve your results.

Communication Exercise

Prepare a comfortable place to sit. Close your eyes and focus on your breathing. Let any thoughts that come into your mind drift out without giving them any attention or attaching any judgment to them.

When you feel your mind is sufficiently still, you may begin by seeing yourself drifting slowly downward through a rainbow. You are slowly floating down through a bright red color. Notice how clear and red it is, extending in all directions as far as you can sense. You may adjust the color to make it a clear, beautiful red if it is muddy or off-color. Enjoy the warm glow and the sense of connection it gives you to the earth.

The next color you encounter on your downward path is orange. Notice the hue of orange. Is it clear and brilliant? The orange makes you conscious of your connection to other living things. Note the width of the band of color compared to the previous one. As you float down, you can adjust the width and color to make it balanced and beautiful.

Next, you enter a sunshiny yellow band. Feel this warm golden glow empowering you. You can modify the color if you wish to make it more clear and consistent throughout.

Now you find yourself entering an emerald green band. This healing color fills you with a sense of love and forgiveness. Make any changes you desire to enhance the clarity or harmony of this beautiful band.

Next you float into a sky blue color. This perfect color fills you with an awareness that you can communicate clearly with all beings, speaking your truth in a loving fashion. As before, you may alter the hue and make any repairs to this band as you travel slowly downward through it.

Then comes a band of the deepest, darkest blue. It surrounds you like a dark night, yet fills you with confidence that you are capable of knowing anything you need to know. The indigo is consistent and clear.

Finally, you enter a violet band of a clear, royal hue. As you float downward, you know that you are now and always connected to the Source of all things, and that connection makes anything possible.

You become aware that you have landed on solid ground. Look around and notice your surroundings. The setting may be a beautiful natural location such as a redwood forest or a sandy beach at the ocean. Whatever place you are represents a secure place to you, a place where you are safe communicating with your animal friends. As you look around, you see a structure. It may be a natural one like a cave or a manmade one like a building.

This structure is your 'center', where you go to talk to animals. As you draw nearer your center, you go through a while light which completely surrounds you. Passing through this glowing white light, you know you are being cleared of blocks, negativity and ego, as well as being protected from any interference or influence, both within and without.

You enter the structure and note your surroundings. The floor, the walls, the furnishings are welcoming and beautiful. They suit your taste perfectly. In front of you is a large stage with very large elevator doors to one side.

A comfortable chair is positioned in front of the stage. This is where you will sit to interview your subjects, who will come out on the stage when you beckon them to a session.

At the back of the stage is a large film screen, on which can be played movies of events, past and present. To one side is a special digital clock that can display date including year.

Go sit in your chair, because it is time to find out who your helpers will be during these communication sessions. You are aware that your guides will help you get better results in your sessions, so you are eager to meet them. You are very relaxed as you ask your helpers to come onto the stage. You count to three. At three, the elevator doors open and your guides walk out onto the stage. Don't stare intently at them, just let the image come to you. It may be a clear visual one, or it may be a fleeting thought or feeling. Remember to let it flow and don't judge or analyze. Your guide may be an angel, a person, a fairy or some type of animal. You may have one or more.

As they approach you on the stage, introduce yourself and thank them for coming. Ask them if they would like to help you in your communication sessions with animals. Their response may be very obvious, or it may slip into your head so quickly you wonder if you have provided it yourself. Whatever you get, go with it.

You may ask them any question you wish, although you may find it easier to stick with 'yes' or 'no' questions at first. If they choose to join you, thank them and invite them to come sit or stand next to you. If they decline to help, thank them anyway and bid them goodbye as they return to the elevator on the count of three and return from whence they came.

When the session is over, thank your helpers and go back the way you came, through the white light and up through the colors of the rainbow in reverse order: violet, indigo, blue, green, yellow, orange and red. Open your eyes and return to the present.

Suggestions

When you talk to animals you will follow the same procedure, only your helpers will greet you at the door as you come in to your center. They will join you as you sit and call out your subjects, and their help will enhance your results.

At the end of the session, you will send your animal subject back into the elevator on the count of three after thanking it for coming, and it will return to its appropriate place.

The screen may be used to run a 'movie' of things that have happened. For example, an animal can show you via the movie screen rather than tell you what happened. You can also examine past lives using the movie screen. Some animals are more open to communicating than others.

Pick an animal you know and love for your first subject. Don't judge your answers. Accept what you get, even if you think you are 'making it up.' You aren't. I like to ask a subject if he or she has anything to say to anyone. Sometimes you can get very interesting and inspiring messages this way. Animals will often want to tell of their love for the person who owns them. Often, they will ask for more of their favorite treats. Sometimes a subject will just leave the session if it doesn't want to talk. We had a tree do that one time. Whatever happens, thank your subject.

You can also talk to inanimate objects using this technique. We have talked to a bike and a stuffed animal successfully this way. The answers to questions posed by students in our class were most interesting and believable. Another thing I have noticed is that you get confirmation for your responses.

Don't be afraid to share them with the person who owns the animal. I once told a woman her horse was a unicorn in a past life even though at the time I felt silly, and I wasn't sure what she would think. She pulled her business cards out. They had a unicorn as her logo. She was also wearing a unicorn pendant. She loved unicorns. It was wonderful confirmation of what her horse had shared.

As with all techniques, practice makes this one more successful. You will find you get more detail the more you practice.

Diet Questionnaire

This is an exercise to give you the opportunity to evaluate how healthy your animal friend's diet is. Answer the following questions.

1. *Are you giving your animal unfiltered tap water to drink?*

2. *Do you buy your animal feeds at the grocery store, pet store or vet's office?*

3. *Check the label of the food. Does the food have any artificial ingredients, such as preservatives or colors or flavor enhancers?*

4. *Are there added supplements such as vitamins and minerals?*

5. *Does the formula have any chelated minerals?* (as opposed to inorganic minerals like -oxides or -carbonates)

6. *Is sugar or another artificial sweetener in the food?* (Corn syrup, molasses and other sweeteners included)

7. *Are there any descriptions of the ingredients, such as 'organic', 'human grade', 'pesticide-free' that indicate an attempt has been made to make the food more healthy?*

8. *Is price your main concern when you buy food for your animals?*

9. *Have you done any reading or research on the different types of feeding programs for your animal, such as at the library or bookstore or on the internet?*

10. *Is your animal the picture of perfect health?* (It never gets sick, looks terrific, has great energy level and has no allergies or behavioral problems)

There are no right or wrong answers to these questions. They are to make you think about what you feed your animal friend.

Notice if you are just listening to commercials or following the crowd, as opposed to taking the time to learn and make your own decision. We are so rushed in our culture, we often make excuses and fail to educate ourselves. Once you become educated, don't become inflexible. Be open to new information (as opposed to fads) as it is presented.

Always go back to asking what Mother Nature intended if you are unsure about whether something is good for your animal.

RESOURCES

Other Books by Maggie & Nigel Percy

We've written over 20 books about dowsing and related topics. If you are interested in dowsing, our course in a book, entitled *Learn Dowsing: Your Natural Psychic Power* is the place to start.

~

Books Relating to Intuitive, Natural Animal Health Care by other authors

The Nature of Animal Healing by Dr. Martin Goldstein, D.V.M., Alfred A. Knopf, New York, 1999. *This is an absolutely terrific book about animal health from the standpoint of a vet who has shifted to a more natural approach.*

Natural Health for Dogs & Cats by Richard H. Pitcairn, D.V.M., Ph.D & Susan Hubble Pitcairn, Rodale Press, Emmaus, PA, 1995. *This is a useful reference guide for the animal owner who prefers holistic treatments.*

Natural Healing for Dogs & Cats by Diane Stein, The Crossing Press, Freedom, CA, 1993. *This is an interesting book that covers not only nutrition and herbs, but acupuncture, massage and muscle testing, among other things.*

A *Modern Horse Herbal* by Hilary Page Self, Kenilworth Press, UK, 1996. *This is, in my opinion, the definitive book on using herbs for horses.*

The Barf Diet by Dr. Ian Billinghurst. Ian Gregory Billinghurst, 2001. *A great guide to raw food diets by an Australian veterinarian.*

Homeopathic Care for Cats and Dogs by Don Hamilton, D.V.M., North Atlantic Books, 2010. *A detailed guide for home care.*

∼

Books on Personality Theory

Gifts Differing by Isabel Briggs Myers, Consulting Psychologists Press, Inc. Palo Alto, CA, 1980. *This is the foundational book on the Myers Briggs Type Indicator, a well-known evaluation system based on the theory of Carl Jung.*

Type Talk by Otto Kroeger and Janet M.Thuesen, Delacorte Press, NY, 1988. *Extensive descriptions of the personality types.*

Please Understand Me by David Keirsey and Marilyn Bates, Prometheus Nemesis Book Company, Del Mar, CA, 1984. *Good descriptions of the sixteen types, but the tests are not too well-crafted in my opinion.*

Life Types by Sandra Hirsh and Jean Kummerow, Warner Books, NY, 1989. *This is an excellent book on the Myers Briggs personality theory.*

ABOUT THE AUTHORS

Maggie and Nigel Percy met online in 2000 through their mutual love of dowsing. They spent the next 20+ years serving a global clientele with dowsing and energy clearing methods. During that time, they presented at many conferences, created the online Dowsing World Summit and gave free dowsing training through videos and articles on their websites. They've written over 20 books on dowsing and metaphysical topics and have published fiction using the pen names Maggie McPhee and Andrew Elgin. To see all their books, visit your favorite online retailer.